Additi<

For *The Measured Breathing*:

Mystery, these poems tell us, continues to reside at the center of every-thing we know about existence . . . Hettich is an earthy fabulist, yet the poems' ingenious transformations read as integral to survival.

—Susan Kelly-DeWitt, author of *Gatherer's Alphabet*

For *Like Happiness*:

Michael Hettich's poems are like grace, like gifts, like the natural world made Technicolor, like Technicolor making the actual world. He is a master of the simile, and in *Like Happiness,* he harnesses a specific and collective memory, the power of myth and allusion, like no one else. His poems give readers a deep happiness, an earned happiness, a happiness decided upon with clarity and wisdom.

—Denise Duhamel, author of *Second Story*

Michael Hettich's persona, vividly alert in a subtropical landscape where the imagination holds its own against the knots and crosses of life, never reduces the world to a formula, poetic or otherwise. Instead, he breaks through, his innocence grounded by experience and with a childlike sense of wonder, into a world "bigger than we are, like happiness, and full of fish that live nowhere else . . ." *Like Happiness* is an amazing work. I'm filled with gratitude for it.

—Alan Davis, author of *So Bravely Vegetative*

For *Systems of Vanishing*:

As a long-time admirer of Hettich's poems, I am thrilled by *Systems of Vanishing,* his most profound and intricate collection to date. Like Joseph Cornell's boxed assemblages, these poems assemble ardent language with splashes of imagery verging on the surreal. Line by line, each poem thus constructs a portal into our subconscious living—as only the finest poetry can do . . ."

—Richard Blanco, author of *How to Love a Country*

These tender, endlessly inventive poems begin in the familiar world, but take us to other realms altogether. Their startling displacements happen so deftly and with such sleight-of-hand that they are nearly invisible. Slowly, as poem after poem reveals "the sadness at the core of every moment," the reader comes to see the impossible as ordinary, and the ordinary as numinous. Michael Hettich's authority, which is both modest and absolutely genuine, compels us to follow him into some wild what-ifs, which make for an exciting ride. His elegy for a lost daughter brought me to tears. The quiet magic of these poems is stunning and profound.

    —Chase Twitchell, author of *Things as It Is*

For *To Start an Orchard*:

In these stunning, fable-like poems, humans turn into animals in transformations that seem utterly natural, if not necessary. There's a merging with wildness, even as wildness is disappearing. The poems themselves seem almost to disappear rather than end, as if they are heading into some trees, or entering the body of a horse.

    —Anne Marie Macari, author of *Heaven Beneath*

Michael Hettich is one of our best and most necessary poets because his dreamlike stories remind us how little we truly see and how often we sleep through the day's deep revelations. This collection—so tightly choreographed and flawlessly written—is like a long poem that shines brighter with each turn of the page . . . *To Start and Orchard* is a call to arms, demanding consciousness, responsibility, and love.

    —Richard Jones, author of *The Minor Key*

For *A Small Boat*:

Worlds fold into worlds, in Michael Hettich's poems, and people into animals and then back again; love spins into ignorance, and passion into wonder; tenderness and beauty blend into cruelty and the shock of hard knowledge. These are lyrical poems of great power and wisdom, and a poet of delicate, ferocious skill. *A Small Boat* is magically fine, and Hettich is a superb poet.

    —Burton Raffel, author of *Beowulf: A New Translation*

There is an immense amount of cargo in *A Small Boat;* it's the kind of book that makes the world bigger.

—David Kirby, author of *More Than This*

For *Flock and Shadow*:

Michael Hettich's poems have consistently provided a quiet phosphorescent glow in the lush garden of contemporary American poetry.

—Nick Carbó, author of *Chinese, Japanese, What are These?*

For *Bluer and More Vast*:

Throughout this stunning collection, life's mysteries are magnified by the poet's vast imagination. Each poem's magical conceit and earthy embrace remind us of our place in the universe and the universe's place within each of us.

—Mia Leonin, author of *Fable of the Pack-Saddle Child*

For *The Mica Mine*:

In this stunningly intuitive and elemental collection, Hettich celebrates the unspoken dialogues of the natural world with linguistic dexterity and fierce transformative details.

—Richard Blanco, author of *How to Love a Country*

The reader will not find headlines in these poems but will be affirmed by the news of our ongoing existence. "This animal would save you if the house were to fall down around you," Hettich tells us, and we want to know that beast. But even more we want to live with Hettich's faith in a world where "our bodies start crying out in languages the trees might dance to."

—Al Maginnes, author of *The Beasts That Vanish*

Also by Michael Hettich

Lathe

A Small Boat

Stationary Wind

Swimmer Dreams

Flock and Shadow

Like Happiness

The Animals Beyond Us

Systems of Vanishing

The Frozen Harbor

Bluer and More Vast: Prose Poems

To Start an Orchard

The Mica Mine

The Halo of Bees

New & Selected Poems
1990–2022

Michael Hettich

Press 53
Winston-Salem

Press 53, LLC
PO Box 30314
Winston-Salem, NC 27130

First Edition

Cover image, "Zayed (Baltimore Series)," Copyright © 2022
by Mark Flowers. Used with permission of the artist.

Author Photo by Colleen Ahern-Hettich

Library of Congress Control Number
2023934268

ISBN 978-1-950413-65-2

for Colleen Ahern-Hettich

*and for all the editors and publishers
who've supported my work through the years*

Acknowledgments

These poems have been selected from the books and chapbooks I published between 1990 and 2021, starting with *A Small Boat* (1990) and ending with *The Mica Mine* (2021). Some of the poems have been revised lightly for this collection. The poems in "The Shape of Moving" were written in 2021 and 2022.

I would like to thank the editors who have supported my work over the years, and particularly the following:

the late Leonard Cirino; the late Robert Bixby; Bob and Susan Arnold; John LeBow; William Slaughter; Richard Jones; the late Scott King; Lynne Knight; Rick Campbell; Richard Mathews; Alan Davis; James Den Boer; Robert Hedin; Gary Metras; Jay Snodgrass; Tom Virgin; Christopher Nelson; Kevin Morgan Watson; Christopher Forrest; Ted Wojtasik

I would be lost without the love of my family: Colleen, Matthew, Emmanuelle, Caitlin, Casey, Owen, and Leo.

I am deeply grateful to Jesse Millner for reading and responding to so many of these poems in their early drafts.

Thanks to Mitchell Kaplan for his support from the beginning and through the years.

Back in 2018, Kevin Morgan Watson agreed to consider an unsolicited manuscript from a poet whose work he didn't know. I am deeply grateful to him for publishing that book (in 2019) and for agreeing to publish this new book. Press 53 is a treasure I'm proud to call my publisher.

Christopher Forrest is a brilliant and deeply sympathetic editor; his editorial insights into some of the poems in the "new poems" section have brought them to fuller life. It has been an honor to work with him again. I hope we will continue to do so in the future—on my own books or on his.

Many thanks to Mark Flowers for the cover art.

"Core" is for Jesse Millner
"I Was" & "The Flood" are for Christopher Forrest
"Song," "Love Poem," "The Dark House" & "Angels in the Trees" are for Colleen Ahern-Hettich

I am grateful to the editors of the publications where the following poems found in "The Shape of Moving" first appeared:

2RiverView, "The Useful Man"

Asheville Poetry Review, "The Daughter"

Boulevard, "Mercy"

Notre Dame Review, "Core"

Cumberland River Review, "Love Poem"

On the Seawall, "The Shape of Moving"

Poetry East, "The Stone Wall," "Stir," "The Ache" & "Pet Dogs and Laughter"

Slant, "The Swan" & "The Blade"

Split Rock Review, "The River" & "Angels in the Trees"

Terrain.org, "Another Kind of Silence" & "Extinctions"

Under a Warm Green Linden, "Gratitude" & "Liminal"

Additional thanks to the people and presses involved in the publication of previous collected works:

Chapbooks:

Looking Out, Moonsquilt Press, 1981

White Birds, MAF Press, 1989

Immaculate Bright Rooms, March Street Press, 1994

Many Simple Things, March Street Press, 1997

Sleeping with the Lights On, Pudding House Publications, 2000

Singing with My Father, March Street Press, 2001

Greatest Hits, Pudding House Publications, 2002

The Point of Touching, John LeBow Letterpress, 2002

Behind Our Memories, Adastra Press, 2003

Many Loves, Yellow Jacket Press/winner of the Yellow Jacket Chapbook Contest, 2007

More Than Gratitude, Longhouse, 2010

Measuring the Days, Mudlark #40, 2010

The Flood, Floating Wolf Quarterly, 2011

The Measured Breathing, Swan Scythe Press/winner of the Swan Scythe Chapbook Contest, 2011

Collaborative/Handmade Art Books:

Home, a collaborative book-arts project pairing five writers and artists, compiled and printed by Tom Virgin/Extra Virgin Press, 2017

The Heartland Project, from The Anderson Center/Southeastern Minnesota Arts Council, 2015

The Ground Beneath Our Feet, 2015

Conversation Too (Convo2), designed, edited and printed by Tom Virgin/ Extra Virgin Press, The Jaffe Center for the Book at Florida Atlantic University, 2014

Collections:

Lathe, Pygmy Forest Press, 1987

A Small Boat, University Press of Florida, 1990

Stationary Wind, March Street Press, 2004

Swimmer Dreams, Turning Point/winner of the Tales Prize, 2005

Flock and Shadow, New Rivers Press, 2005

Like Happiness, Anhinga Press, 2010

The Animals Beyond Us, New Rivers Press, 2011

Systems of Vanishing, University of Tampa Press/winner of the *Tampa Review* Prize, 2014

The Frozen Harbor, Red Dragonfly Press/winner of the David Martinson/ Meadowhawk Prize and a Florida Book Award, 2017

Bluer and More Vast: Prose Poems, Hysterical Books, 2018

To Start an Orchard, Press 53, 2019

The Mica Mine, St. Andrews College Press, winner of the 2020 Lena Schull Book Award, 2021

Contents

Selections from *Immaculate Bright Rooms, Many Simple Things, Singing with My Father, Greatest Hits, Beyond Our Memories, The Point of Touching* & *Many Loves*

Selections from *Stationary Wind* & *Swimmer Dreams*

Selections from *Flock and Shadow*

Selections from *Like Happiness*

Selections from *The Mica Mine*

After all a poem is made up not of the things of which it speaks directly but of things which it cannot identify and yet yearns to know.

—W.C. Williams in a letter to Denise Levertov, January 6, 1954

The Shape of Moving

Core

The hawk in the white pine shivers, hunched
into itself like a state of being

we might think had vanished
if we've been playing
too long with our gadgets, or making arrangements
to assure our perfect happiness

sometime in the future. The wind that tossed
cut-down trees
remains a ghost
inside our furniture, like the antique
notion of a soul, and ancient tides

drew the swirls in the stones that line
our paths. Scars that mark the seasons

our ancestors lived,
etched like tree rings
into the secrets we don't even know
we're keeping; a dream that woke us to forget,

a blue that dazzles the sky as only
nothing can do, in the morning.

Driving Home

The man at the edge of the highway is singing
to the passing cars, and though we can't hear him,
cocooned as we are in our speed, we can see
it's a bellowing trumpet song, like a burst
of grackles from a gun-shocked maple, up into
the sky. There's a dog crouched in the switchgrass
as though hiding there, and what looks like a baby
in a bassinet of homemade design, and now
just as that little group shrinks from the rear-view,
a car pulls off to give them a ride
I suppose, or maybe some money, and we
resume the conversation we were having, about
the lives we are living and the lives we might
have lived, had we turned different corners, and I think
of his child there, dozing or maybe being licked
in the face by that shaggy old dog. I imagine
that baby as a grown-up remembering his dad
singing for a ride. And I think of my own father
singing to himself as he poured his morning coffee
then carrying it upstairs to dress for work,
barefoot, though the house was chilly—it was winter—
feeling the pleasure of a moment to himself
before the day's rush and tumble, not knowing
somehow I was watching him, if only in my own
fondest recollection of the songs he loved to sing,
"Round Midnight," or maybe "I Cover the Waterfront"—
songs he'd first heard in the Navy during
the war. And as we exit, these songs
start playing through my head; I hear myself whistling
softly, wondering what that man was singing
to the cars and his child, maybe opera, something
dramatic I think from the way he gestured
and turned his face up to the sky.

Stir

Sometimes a breeze will pick up between
two people who don't know each other
and blow between them while they stand in line
or sit in a classroom. The breeze feels pleasant
as it enters the folds in their clothing but they don't
pay it much attention. It's a mammal-scented
breeze reminiscent of mushrooms and rotting
leaves in a pile at the edge of the path
that leads to a bend in the creek where you sometimes
take off your clothes for a dip. You sit naked
in the sun until you've dried off. Then you walk home feeling
as fresh as a rock. Those birds will never judge you
but the deer that come to that pool to drink
will smell your body for days until
the first heavy rain. Look at them standing there
soaked through but still so elegant as they
bend to rip out the grass or nibble
at the leaves that keep your pool hidden
like this breeze that's so private you don't even know
what you're feeling, as now for the first time you notice
her hair, the way she unfolds her delicate
hands and sighs as she buttons her sweater,
shivering a little from the chill.

An Ordinary Morning

As I step out into the morning, holding
a plate of food scraps for the compost, I glance up
the hillside, into the leafless trees,
to see a huge deer standing still, watching me
watch him, so I hold my breath and try
to still my thoughts too, as if he might somehow
see them flickering through me, and bolt.
My wife is still sleeping in the house. There's a whiff
of winter in the air, and I'm wearing only
the clothes I slept in. I wish I could call her
out, to see this deer—or join her
in the warm bed without disturbing her dreams,
like a memory that actually matches the moment
it plays, over years, through the mind. When I move
slightly, the big deer shivers and tightens,
and I see for the first time a score of other deer
moving through the woods. Some of them seem to be
floating up into the bare trees, up
where the slope is steep; others look like
bushes with brown leaves moving in a light breeze
although the morning is still. And then,
like a silence that echoes in itself, they run
in one long exhalation followed by a pause
before the next breath, as my wife leans out
to ask why I'm standing in the frigid early morning,
without shoes, holding a plate of stale food
as though I were making some sort of offering.
So I point up the ridge to the trees and silence,
put the plate down, and turn to come in,
shivering a little, for the first time, from the cold.

Mercy

How many days, she asked, will it take you
to take apart the engine? And how many weeks
will it take you to build the train you promised
to take us away on, to visit the towns
we've imagined being happy in but have never visited,
those villages we know so well from the books
you read out loud, while I looked out the window
at the dull street we live on, in this dull town
full of dog-faced women in raincoats and men
whose bellies emerge from their golf shirts.
When will you fix the lights in the bedroom
and get the mice out of the plumbing?
We could climb up the sides of the mountains we've seen
on our calendars; we could breathe the thin air
until the world thinned too, yet still we'd keep hiking,
pulling each other up above the tree line,
then sliding quickly down to a café we remember
from that book we loved so much we never
finished reading it; we kept turning
the pages back, rereading favorite passages.
Flushed from our adventure, we'd sit drinking wine
and finishing the story, then closing the book
and slipping it back on the shelf. But the shelf
is covered in mouse droppings, and the roof is leaking
again now from this incessant rain
and we don't have buckets and no one else is home
in this entire town, so no one will answer
when we knock on their doors for help; we'll keep running
from front door to front door hoping for mercy,
laughing a little as we splash,
and maybe even taking off our clothes, to marvel
at how pale our bodies have grown.

Shade

1.

My mother climbed the rickety ladder
into that huge crabapple tree,
feeling for worm-free apples we could taste
and make something out of, applesauce or pie.

The day was cool. My mother was singing,
hidden in the tree-shade. I was singing too.

She threw an apple down at me
and laughed to watch me dodge and shriek,

then stepped off into the tree and seemed
to *really* disappear,
which scared me—just a boy—

so I climbed up into
the apple-scented shade
to find her sitting on a limb, holding
apples in her skirt with both hands—how would she
climb down that way?—and crying softly.

Her legs were scratched and streaked with dirt
and her delicate manicured feet were bare.

2.

These many years later, I see her standing
at the open kitchen window
watching the first birds of spring at her feeder,
trying to remember their names, and wishing
she could vanish without
going anywhere, move
out of her body like a breath does, into open air.

She thinks about the distance those small birds have flown
and since I'm still her son, I see her turn away,

I see her turn away now and move through the house
touching her furniture, talking to the pictures
on the walls—not the photographs of family arranged
like a bouquet across her bedroom walls

but the paintings of flowers standing rigid in their vases,
a three-masted schooner moving out to open sea.

The Wound

Another morning she knew how to speak
whatever languages anyone else
was speaking, wherever she travelled, whomever—
whatever—she spoke to. Eventually these languages
grew cramped inside her. They rubbed and jostled
each other. Their friction started to burn off
the secrets where she'd lived

until smoke filled the sky of her memories, fire
burned down the house of her earliest days.
In the front yard, her parents floated up and away
like ashes, to drift down in a distant country

with another language, where a girl like her
woke up to an ordinary morning
and knew something was wrong. Still, she lay there
listening to her mother putter in the kitchen
and her dad whistle softly as he headed off to work.

The Wind Chime

Those mornings we woke before ourselves
and walked through the house singing in breaths
meant to measure some other kind of waking,
a need we'd tried to rid ourselves of
by burying who we'd once been, to forge
who we really were now, in harmony. Then,

as the day lightened, we woke again, to broken glass—
who knew where it came from—across the barefoot floor,
so we talked about the feathers in our memories, the downy
feathers we'd hid beneath our clothes;
we talked about orchards full of ripe fruit
that would never fall, gardens of sweet smells
we could taste by breathing,

and the silence of the future, which would always be ideal
until it was the present. Then, as we swept up
the glass and broken pottery, the broken-spined books
of poetry, the fur-tufts from the cave-drawn animals
whose eyes we felt watching us now, we wondered

who was living in the wind; we wondered
why we'd made this skin except
to thicken our nerves, and as we worked
to pretend the fire still burning at the back
of our eyes might actually light a path
through the dark, we thought we heard a bell
in the distance, a wind chime that quivered the air
and made us sit more still, to listen.

Song

While my wife spent days on her knees, pulling
English ivy, I cut paths through rhododendron
thickets, then lugged the cut branches down
the hill to be mulched. Later, toward evening,
we sat out in the driveway and watched the sky
darken for bats, then stars, and when
the dark was full, we felt our way inside,
lay down together, and dreamed: *Come out now,*

my love, to follow these paths we've made
that lead to other paths, and others, until
we find ourselves standing by a pool, naked,
slipping into the water that's full
of phosphorescence, like the stars; our bodies
will glow as we swim out to the middle, and stand
on the sand there, heads in the sky, telling
stories we wouldn't have remembered otherwise:

The wind through the trees as we sang to our children
so they'd fall asleep, the ways that wind slipped in
sometimes to our bedroom
and took our sleeping children
up into the trees, still sleeping. We climbed
for what seemed like years, to gather them gently
and climb down, careful not to wake them, or fall.

We remember we lived so silently then.
We remember we walked out once beyond town
and held each other gently and disappeared together,
singing like the rain against the thirsty ground,
singing like a shadow does, flying.

The Stone Wall

I am coming to the end of something, I can feel it
like a bone that was useful in the past, that kept me
standing upright but has turned into a toothpick
or a splinter dissolving in my blood—and although
I didn't notice the changes at first,
recently I've found myself turning corners carefully,
holding my shoulders as though I were naked
even when I'm fully dressed, even in a winter coat,
without that lost bone. And so I woke at dawn
because someone had left me, someone I'd lived
inside of. I got up and walked through the dark house
bumping into furniture as though I were gathering
flowers. Under our feet there is water
moving, always, and animals that breathe
all that falls away. So when the morning brightened,
I gathered the stones I'd collected on my journeys
and kept on the windowsill. I carried them outside
to make a small stone wall, to remember something precious,
a stone wall without function, hidden in the grass.

I Was

walking down the hill in my usual daze
when a car I didn't recognize pulled up
and a man I'd never seen before
stepped out. He was crying and laughing
at the same time, arms opened wide, and I thought
maybe I should just keep walking. The car
hummed along beside us, like an embarrassed child
as this old guy started talking, too quickly, in a voice
I recognized faintly but couldn't quite place.
He said he was amazed: I hadn't changed at all,
though I know full well I've changed almost completely.
Still, his reassurance made me like him more,
so I hugged him back, and tried to cry too, and laugh—
after all he must have been a close friend, or a relative,
nearly a brother to love me so enthusiastically.
And who was I, after all? *I've been looking for you,*
he said then, *for so many years I've lost count,*
and I've found you so many times, everywhere I go—
but you've always slipped away like a dream. How
the hell have you been? And so I start to tell him
stories I remember about myself
and some things I thought I'd forgotten, and then
some other things I just feel like making up,
not lies exactly but versions of a person
like me who's not me and never lived at all.
He laughs and tells me that's why he's so happy
to have found me after all these years, that his life
has been like that too—just amazing yet somehow
not present at all. Then he leans back into his car
and drives off, leaving a swirl of dust
which glitters in the afternoon sunlight
as it settles back down into silence.

Certain Forms of Love

I could be the number of days you still have
to live, or the ancient trees swaying
in the dreams that haunt you; maybe I'm the old dog
sniffing the sidewalk for a clue to where
his master's gone. I might be that disappeared

master, or the pigeons cooing by the fountain,
pecking at the breadcrumbs
an old woman threw there,

or the kind of breeze that knows how to slip in
between things: the bricks of a house, let's say;
layers of clothing; or even the moments
of a life lived by watching.

Out on the street, people are turning
into photographs, smiling as though they were already
ghosts—and when my face is caught
in a mirror, I see the mask of an animal,
almost extinct, like certain forms

of love. I call it a rare species
of hunger, imagine a wing in its mouth,
a tracing of blood on the snow—

then I turn from myself to look out the window
and watch it slink off through the trees.

The Blade

Do you see the birds, you asked me, flying up there now,
those tiny dots of darkness? They are turning to air
as they fly, drifting down across our shoulders
like nothing if *nothing* had substance—like dust.

Another day you told me I just want to sleep
as you opened a window and leaned out into city air
gritty with darkness of another kind, another kind
of dust that hummed with all that had been
forgotten, all we pretended to remember.

On the roof across the alley a flock of pigeons
fretted, then swirled up into the sky—

and that was enough to turn you away
from the window, hold yourself out to me, and smile,
though everything had already been lost, you said,
to the days that would follow, each of them sharper,
leaner than those that had come before,

until there would be nothing but a kind of *blade*
you called it, and smiled. You were not an old woman
you reminded me again, and you loved me, if that
made any difference. And I do think it must have,

though I don't know why. When I kissed you goodbye,
the scent of the powder on your cheek made me
gag a little, because I couldn't cry—

and you looked up at me, straight into my eyes,
and I saw you in there, for a moment.

The Useful Man

Now I think of him walking the length of a train
that moves through a landscape he's never seen before.
I watch as he leans to look out, or balances
between the cars to catch a glimpse
of that unfamiliar country. Then he turns and walks
back to his seat, past the forward-looking faces
of the strangers who pretend not to watch him.

And when the train sighs and pulls into a station,
after many hours, he steps down, crying,
forgetting the suitcase full of his diaries,
records of the precious lives he lived where he's come from,
that country whose name he's already forgotten.

The sidewalk gleams like a river on a sunny
afternoon as he walks beyond the houses
to the fields where crows are ripping off the clothes
of the old men propped up on scaffolds, the old
straw-filled geezers who were hired to scare
the birds off and are clearly not doing their jobs.

Maybe he can go out and lift them from their racks
and maybe he can climb up there himself, to see
if his body might be any more effective than theirs.
After all, he came here to be useful.

The Shape of a Song

1.

This morning, when I woke before first light,
I felt that breathtaking strangeness of *nothing*,
its closeness all around me, in the darkness.

When I lay back down beside my sleeping wife
to lose myself again, she woke
for a moment to ask, *are you all right, my love?*

And I didn't have to answer, after all,
since she'd already hugged me, and fallen back to sleep.

2.

What is the weight of blue in the morning
just before sunrise, when the last snow
of the season lies at the edge of the woods,
starting to glow with first light?

What is the weight of the moment that wakes you
to get up and walk to the window, to watch
the mountains step gradually
out of the darkness,

and what is the weight of your breath, of the life
inside you, the weight of the years you've lived,
the weight of the love you've shared and the love
you've denied, the weight of the love you've received

without question? Sometimes we feel we might
remember the breath we drew the moment
our bodies became *bodies*—that feeling of being
loved so completely we were something like silence
just being shaped into song.

The Secret

On the highway to town, I realize the dead dog
lying in the swale might actually be
a coyote—something in the shape of its body,
the coarseness of its fur—and though I keep driving,
later I wish I'd pulled over, maybe
dragged the dead animal off into the bushes

but I was hurrying somewhere, half-listening
to the radio chattering news, or singing
to the empty car—some old song I'd happened
to hear in the grocery store, The Carpenters or Billy Joel—
cheesy, sentimental stuff I love

like a secret you've kept for so long you hardly
remember what you promised not to tell, or the better kind
of secret that lives outside language: the smell
of a pillow someone you loved slept on
beside you for years, dreaming and tossing
sometimes in her sleep, and sometimes turning,

half awake, to wrap her arms around
your sleeping body, then falling contentedly
back into dreams, her freshly-washed hair
pressed into her pillow, and filling the darkness
with the scent of blossoming flowers.

The River

I'm taking a pause from the person I've been
for most of my life and starting to enter
the man I've been only occasionally, even
the man I've only pretended to be—
a stranger I've hardly imagined.

My wife has decided to do the same.
We've agreed to try out our new selves and meet
back here in a few days, to talk things over,
perhaps make some permanent adjustments.

Our children might be strangers soon.
Our old dog already ignores us.

The river that runs by our house has been rising
for weeks. We've been cleaning out our closets,
tossing things into the swirl:
old books we thought we should love, classics
that only bored us, as they've bored everyone
for centuries; photo albums full of squinting strangers;
dress shoes that pinched; overstuffed pillows
that made our necks stiff. And then, one morning,

a herd of deer tried to swim across to our side.
So many hungry animals have been swept away.

Even our faces in the mirror seem
to have been swept away now, by that rising river
and by our yearning. I can only be naked,
though I'm trying to locate the clothes I wore
when I was a man who sported perfect teeth
and a full head of hair, the kind who tells the truth
when he lies—or vice versa, I can't remember now,
though I'm sure it must matter to someone.

Another Kind of Silence

Sometimes the world grows louder, you realize,
just as the day falls still
and insects whose names you'll never know
start screaming and laughing, scraping their wings,
then falling silent. It's as though there were some

technology that could capture your dreams
and throw them on a screen, to show you to yourself
and confuse you more deeply, you who are not
alone but live in solitude, never
seeing anyone but yourself, even

when you are talking with your friends and family,
even when you're moving through a crowd, thinking

Everything is wild at its core, even
half-asleep evenings in front of the TV,
even listless afternoons shopping
for knickknacks, or food. And food is especially
wild. Just think of all those apples and grains
of rice, just think of that wine
ripening as grapes in the bright sun of some
foreign country, the bees and even

the bats zig-zagging through the gloaming, singing
as they feast—another kind of silence:

music your ears are not built to hear,
like the roots of these trees, humming as they soak up
the puddles that have deepened for so many days
you hardly remember how the sunlight feels
on your body, how it makes you squint
and see things differently, the way it makes everything

waver and shimmer, like a mirage
you walk toward, never arriving.

The Ache

We don't mean to come to the end of our lives
before they come to us, but we do, she says,
sitting beside me in the crowded waiting room,
waiting to be called in. I nod as though I understand,
which I do, but I don't say anything since

my teeth have been aching. It's a small pain, of course,
in the vast world of hurt, but distracting nonetheless,
since I'd rather be outside, paying attention
to the butterflies we see in this season, as of course
I want to know which birds are flying south

or north, outside this office. I want
to listen to their songs, as though by listening
I might reverse the direction of extinctions
harrowing our planet, though I know that's only
a lazy man's dream. Now she's fiercely brushing

her hair, grunting as she pulls. She shakes
her head and smiles, getting strands of hair
all over my sweater, as everyone else
stares at the TV, or leafs through ancient magazines.
And when she starts humming, too loudly not

to be trying to say something urgent, I look up
from my phone, I forget myself
for a moment, and smile—as though that were enough.
Of course it's not. But she smiles back anyway,
as though she were forgiving me, just as my name is called.

The Shape of Moving

Someone traces the wind back to where it started,
back before the dinosaurs, and wins a big prize

and ends up committing suicide somewhere
out in the desert, which has been getting hotter

by the day. *It's where the wind ends,* his note says,
and no one finds him for so long he's been eaten

by insects and vultures—all but his bones
and cap, stained by his sweat—just enough

to identify his DNA. And as I'm reading his story,
the woman I love most in the world comes into

the kitchen and tells me her life has been wasted,
then looks out the window to marvel at the blooming

flowers no one has planted, the buzzing
bees no one has summoned. Yesterday

a neighbor stopped by to tell us the yellowjacket
wasps were swarming through the woods, stinging

every human they could find, and when we wondered
why they were so restive, he ventured a theory

that all the new houses were disturbing the soil
where the wasps hibernate, and he wondered if they thought,

somehow—if wasps think at all—that they might
sting us away? When he left, we packed up

a bottle of wine and some glasses and walked up
to the man-made lake at the edge of the woods

a mile or so away. We sat and watched the evening
blow across the water like a small bird might do

before landing in the trees on the other side, to sing.
And so we drank our wine and listened for a while,

then slowly walked back through the darkness.

Extinctions

In the backyard we stood in the twilight and watched
thousands of birds flying south.
We wondered if anyone knew who they were,
and we wondered how they knew where to go, whether
we'd ever have any sense of where
we were or were going. Of course we were just children.

In the house, our parents were turning on lights
and walking around with purpose, talking
loudly about things we couldn't understand,
things they would *shush* when we walked into the room.

We could see their shapes through the living room window
as we stood there looking up into the sky
at those thousands and thousands of small lives, flying
somewhere, yelping and singing to each other
as they flew. And when it was too dark to see
we turned and went inside for dinner.

Pet Dogs and Laughter

I woke up alone in an unfamiliar city
and spent the day walking, getting lost and trying
to find my way back. I spoke to no one as I walked
to wear myself away so I could fall asleep.
My face in the mirror was the same one I'd lived with
for so many years I hardly knew another,
though I realized I hadn't always been the man
I saw now, so familiar I couldn't really see him,
another kind of stranger. I'd been a young man, of course,
and before that I'd been the idea of a person
who would move through the world, the idea of a wound
who might become human, like the wind becomes a tree.
But there were no trees here, in this city I didn't even
know the name of, though I'd wandered its streets,
watched its citizens and children and tasted
its strange cuisine, which I'd never learn to eat
without remembering the food I'd come from,
the food I'd grown up on. I'd tasted their wine.
I'd even gotten drunk and wandered down into the subway
where it was almost too dark to see, where trains
screeched into the station to wait there, empty
and throbbing. Too frightened to climb onboard,
I thought about it often, imagining the neighborhoods
those sleek trains might fly to, at the edge of the city,
a storybook place full of pet dogs and laughter
where maybe I could step off and be myself again,
whoever that might be now. And as I walked around
and around I thought about myself there. I sat
on benches pretending to be perfectly content
while I dreamed of stepping down from that train and waiting
for someone to welcome me home.

Gratitude

1.

The murmur of rain as I lay in my childhood
bed between dreams and dreaming with someone
moving through another part of the house
maybe singing probably not
the window glass cool as I looked out eager
to go out while everyone thought I was still
sleeping to be drenched in solitude yellow
slicker on or maybe just pajamas after all
I was just a boy surrounded by my privacy
walking unseen to the mucky creek I loved most
when the tide was low in the silence of that rain
then coming back soaked now home to the warm house
where everyone was sleeping still with the clatter
of a train across the harbor pulling the morning
free of its darkness pulling the curtain
of rain aside full of people looking out I knew them
I thought like I knew my own body chilly now
as I took off my jacket and pjs and slipped back
into bed while the radiator clanked and my brother
laughed from his own bed across the dim room
and asked if I'd made the geese fly up
from the rushes or let them keep sleeping

2.

And when the storm had passed, the day smelled like wind
across a wide meadow I remembered like we almost
remember a dream, or the story of a boy
who hid in the grasses that were taller than he was

until whoever was looking for him
had vanished and he stepped out into the day
to set off down the road, on a quest to find something
I can't remember now, though I do know the book

recounted his adventures, which I loved, since I needed
to get lost myself, to feel myself fade
from who I was supposed to be, into my not-quite
and never-mind dream life: I'd watched my brother swim

out beyond the breakers, too far to swim back in,
but I hadn't swum out there to save him. Instead
I'd made up a song, a spell to turn the tide,
and pretended it had worked when he drifted back to shore

to wake up in the bunk bed above me, singing
another song we both loved, "Blowin' in the Wind,"
as we danced around the bedroom, laughing, like a secret
we would never tell, dancing and singing

together, sleep-tousled, wearing only the underpants
we'd slept in, windows open to the green air
of summer, with someone calling someone else's name
up and down the street, so we didn't have to listen

and could just keep on dancing and singing, laughing
at the way we were dancing and singing, until
our mother called up to us: *come down to breakfast*
and we realized we were hungry, nearly starving.

Love Poem

If every word is a path, and every
silence a glimpse of the sky, we're walking
farther now, under more fragrant trees,
though we move more slowly, resting by the side
of the road, waving to strangers and old friends
as they drive off to work, or to foreign countries
where no one knows them. And if we sit long enough
to gather our strength, and sit with that strength
until it becomes who we are now, we start
to hear the weather moving through the trees,
a distant waterfall, or a snake gleaming
through the leaves. We also listen to the birds
begin to forget we are here; we hear
the wilder mammals, who think like we do,
and see us as ghosts now. *I can only hold you*
I say to myself, which is almost the same
as speaking to you, *but I can't take your pain
away, and I want someone bigger than we are
to cover us both like a blanket, or fill us
with a music to sing over everything else
we're feeling.* Soon we will get up and walk
a bit farther, looking for a clearing with a lake
as warm as our blood; we'll swim out into
the middle, to find its shallow core
where we'll stand with only our heads poking out
and feel the minnows nibbling our legs
and laugh at their gentle tickling, then turn
and swim back to shore, just a few strokes away,
to watch as the evening fills the spaces
between things; we'll listen to the night creatures
wake up and sing until morning.

The Dark House

Trust the simple things, she said then, to lead us
through this dark house, hands outstretched to feel
what we can't see, as we touch a wall,
a table, or a chair we can sit in and wait
for morning. Maybe we'll talk of small pleasures

or just listen to each other's breath. We might seem to see
dreams flicker through our open eyes,
though it needs to be darker, even darker than it is now,
and they only flicker briefly. Don't be scared.
We can hold hands and listen for our heartbeats, and maybe

if we can locate a window in the wall,
we can open it and let the outside darkness
rush in with its clarity and wildness; we can sit here
talking of what we imagine must live
out there, waiting for first light—like we are—

or moving through the dark like the moon does, pulling
the tides inside us, oceans we might even
swim out in, naked and warm, until morning
when we'll be out of sight, so far from shore
our lives there might go on without us.

The Daughter

The trees were suddenly alive with birds
whose gnarled little faces made her remember
a long-ago painting she'd seen once, she thought,
in a library book. But these birds were *actual*,
singing at her now, *go home before dark*.

And dark was a man, she knew that, someone
who fixed things for her mother, broken pipes
or closet doors, an old man who kept
his own small animals
hidden in his clothes,
hamsters and mice; you could see them peeking out
when he leaned to adjust the pipes beneath
the kitchen sink, humming and smelling

like fur. Her mother thanked him, smiling
and he shuffled off into the basement, where he lived.
At night she imagined him down there, with his
mice in their cages, running on their little wheels.

In the kitchen the water still dripped from the faucet
and her mother still cried, though she thought no one noticed.

The moon would be out now, a smudge above the trees
where all those little birds with old people's faces
were sleeping. If she cried out they'd wake
and take off, calling her name as they flew.

The Swan

That morning a swan was caught in the ice,
far out. A pack of dogs had gathered,
yapping and teasing, keeping their distance
as the huge bird snapped at them, hissed, and lunged,
fell quiet a moment, then beat its huge white wings.

Her dad lit a cigarette, took a sip from his thermos,
slid out over the thinner ice, holding
his arms out like a circus performer
crossing the high wire, and shooed the dogs away.

Then he crouched down and watched, and when the swan
lay still, he walked back to where she waited, holding
the line in the waning dark, leaning
over the hole he'd chopped an hour earlier.

They walked home at first light and woke up her mother,
had a big breakfast and laughed that they hadn't
caught anything, as usual—

but that didn't really matter. By evening, fresh snow
had started to fall; it swirled and moaned
while she lay in bed, inside her own pale body,
and listened to her parents moving through the house,

talking softly and turning off the lights,
then lying down together in the darkness.

Liminal

When she slept with the window open, she'd listen
to the insects and night creatures singing and feel
her body, potent beyond what she knew

and she'd listen to the night train moving across
the distant horizon. She'd imagine the passengers
sitting there, dreaming a little, looking
out the window at the dark which reflected

only their own pale faces, distorted
by the grime and the lights from the towns the train
moved through. Sometimes as she lay there

on her back, in the deep breaths just before sleep,
she could see the sparks from the wheels of that train
fly out from its engine, up into the night,
like sparklers at a picnic on a warm summer evening

or stars in some universe that was just being born
as that train moved on through the darkness.

Angels in the Trees

My wife drapes her drying dresses across the mountain laurel branches; she forgets them there all night, and in the morning, walking out, she thinks for a moment she sees a choir of angels standing at the edge of the woods, watching her. It's only her own dresses, full of dew now and smelling clean as snow. One of her dresses is hanging deeper in the woods, higher in the branches; we don't know how it got there. I carry the wooden ladder back and prop it as best I can inside the flurry of twigs and leaves, and I climb up carefully and carry it down. It's covered in eager little inch worms, so we hang it in the sun until they've slipped to the ground on their strands of filament. Then she puts it on, this dress I bought her many years ago in a foreign country—she'd stopped walking and gasped when she saw it in the window; it reminded her of something or someone she didn't quite remember. And it fit her perfectly. The salesperson nodded with a smile that looked genuine and we tried to tell her how grateful we were, but we couldn't speak the language, and anyway the woman had turned to someone else by then. My wife looks even more beautiful now than she did when she first tried the dress on, as she once again remembers what she can't put into words and walks around smiling, barefoot in the sun.

The Flood

It's a song about a river, or something like a river,
that flows through the city, a river that floods
yards and parks and streets

to gather all the stray dogs and cats, and carry them
down to the ocean where it lets them
turn back into the wildness.

There are fish in that river that look like fists
and fish with the faces of babies.
There are fish like love when it first alights
on your shoulder to whisper someone's else's secrets.

Other fish swim into houses where lovers
wake startled in the middle of the night
to find themselves wearing someone else's jewelry,

bracelets that glisten like ice-crusted snow
on an evening when a train full of weary commuters

stops to wait as a herd of deer
crosses the tracks between these woods and those,
walking daintily across the snow—

the scene is like a sudden glimpse into the silence
between thoughts, a breath that takes a long time,

until finally one man steps down from the train
in his thin suit and dress shoes and shoos the deer
off the tracks, across the icy field
so the train can move on through the darkness.

Selections from
A Small Boat

Your Mother Sings

Your mother sings
an old song as she
hangs the wash. She looks around—

And when she is sure
no one is watching
(but you are watching) she lets the pigeons

she keeps at the bottom of her laundry basket
fly free—
Each has a note

in its beak. And now a pigeon
flies in your window, dies at your feet.
The note says: *I live alone, please*

come, please help me. But she doesn't live
alone, your mother
is downstairs now

moving pots and pans, starting
dinner, singing
a song she sang,

you remember, when you couldn't sleep.
You hear her down there
singing. You see the pigeon on the floor.

White Birds

1.

I'm not quite myself here, where pets of all sorts hang from
dripping trees, in fishing nets and hammocks, bleating, turning
in the breeze. Dogs, horses, goats, cats—all bleating in voices
I recognize. And I keep calling their names: *Here, Roger,* and
a little dog kicks violently in his net: *Here Old Black,* and the
blind horse tries to rear.

I am wandering with you, my true love. The tips of my fingers
are bleeding inside my white gloves. You look beyond me, your
face and body suddenly a swan, long neck flexing to grab and
pull me off the dock into the polished water I reflect in, dressed
all in white.

Swans change to clouds as I look across the water.

2.

As kids we used square nets to catch minnows to catch snappers
with. We spilled them all over the peeling dock and watched
them flip-flop—so cool and clean. Best to bait them still alive.

My friends liked to throw knives into the mass of them. *Thunk*
of the heavy fishing blade into the dock. Half-fish still flip-flop.
We bend close, squinting.

I hated baiting minnows, hated catching fish.

Sometimes when I caught a fish I'd cut my line, tell my friends a
snapper had broken it. Nights, waiting for sleep, I'd imagine the
silver beauty swimming through dark water, filament trailing
phosphorous behind him. I'd lie in bed listening to my parents
move through the house, mumbling, rearranging furniture,
saying what could have been my name, a leather sound, over
and over. Until I wasn't there.

The world is so different now, who could compare?

3.

It was late afternoon. We were waiting for my father. There was a tiger, she said, in the closet, way back behind everything. We went back there, down a damp trail, stood watching this huge flame pace back and forth behind a window. No, it was a cage; I'm sure I remember daring my hand through the bars. A yellow warmth. The closet glowed. Mother's face looked harsh in the tiger light, but she turned to me, smiling. Smell of candle wax, of wet nylon stockings . . .

Then she smoked a cigarette and cried softly, smiling down at me.

When we came out it was still only early afternoon.

Then a jet passed, very low and fast. We got down on our knees and covered our heads, my mother and I, the way I'd been taught at school. I showed her the proper way to kneel there. Then the jet was gone. The air smelled like glass. We stood up and smiled at each other. She hugged me.

I smelled something cooking, something Father loved to eat.

4.

Hurt birds thrashing by the side of the highway
as I hurry to work, radio blaring.

*

My love, another lover took you deep into the woods. And then, like the click of a perfect lid, he disappeared.

The ground, you told me, was littered with feathers.

The wind
was a wall.

*

These days, it seems, we hardly talk at all.

5.

The skeleton of a shore bird. Gestures that contain a life.

His granddaughter grew wings she told only him about.
She sat on his lap and listened to the same story
he told every night. But tonight, something
kept climbing over the edge of his ribs
to look over her shoulder, into the book
he was pretending to read.

She was smiling, warm. Grandpa smelled good,
like snow and tobacco. They both had a secret.

His original granddaughter had flown away.
This beautiful girl was just a stand-in, a shade.

Outside, the perfume the city fathers
had decided to use to make the air
more "like it used to be" hit the closed window
and continued on, humming an old song
I'm sure you'd recognize:

Now I lay me down to sleep . . .

(Hurt birds thrashing by the side of the road.)

I pray the lord my soul to keep . . .

(My love, someone took you
deep into the woods.)

If I should die . . .

(Gestures that contain a life)

before
I wake, I
pray . . .

6.

Clouds change to swans across your eyes.

Hands

Today thousands
of envelopes filled
with tiny hands
are passing through the mail.

It is a sunny
day, and all
these small hands sweat
in their mailman's bags.

These are the hands
of the skunks, squirrels,
raccoons that have now
become so valued

for their strangeness, for their
resemblance to ours.

Deep in the woods
there are still small animals
with all four hands.
They hide well. And all

around the edges,
close to our houses,
many walk on stumps.
They don't walk far.

We feed them scraps
from our dinners, and they
grow fat and sleek.
They sleep without fear.

Their hands will last
forever now.

Selections from
Immaculate Bright Rooms
Many Simple Things
Singing with My Father
Greatest Hits
Beyond Our Memories
The Point of Touching
Many Loves

Light

For over a year, when I was a boy,
night never fell. We lived inside closets
for the darkness, or underneath
beds, and we grew
deliriously tired. Eventually we dreamed
while we went about our lives, while we talked to each other,
and lived a kind of double life, dreaming and waking
at the same time, even when we drove our cars,
even when we talked or touched each other.
Gradually, we almost forgot about darkness,
in less than a year. Night creatures starved.
Crops grew heavy in half the normal season;
children went to school double time, and we worked
just to do something, and we grew thin just living,
and we grew old more quickly,
bleached pale from all that light.

Behind Our Memories (excerpt)

A small dog lives inside a lonely man, in a little room
built into the intestines like a tree house in a tree.
At night while the man sleeps, the dog keeps faithful watch
in the absolute darkness; he barks at all suspicious
noises: the gurgle and grunt of digestion,
the moan, the cough, the rasp of troubled sleep.
Some nights the man is awakened by the barking
from deep inside his body, so he lets his dog out
to sniff his apartment, to show him all's well.
And the good dog never wants to go back inside
when the man smiles and whispers, raises his shirt
and pats his hairy belly—but he is just
a dog, after all, so he does what he is told.
He likes being in there when his master walks
through the city, singing softly, or talking to himself.
He's comforted by the lulling rhythms of the man's walk,
and he dreams, while he sits in that man-dark, of wolves
and foxes, vast fields he could run across
until he grew powerful, and smart as pure hunger,
until he might swallow a human, keep him
inside his body, which is like a vast woods
before any stories we've ever heard were told,
before anybody had walked across the snow,
before there was *before*. And there he'd let his human free.

*

As dusk fell, my children and I walked along the train tracks,
through a run-down neighborhood, across a black, shallow
river in which manatees lolled. We watched the wind breathe
butterflies and tiny birds; we watched a kingfisher shoot its
hatchet body at its own shadow, skim the water lightly, circle
up and again. That night I dreamed I'd given birth to a baby
whose umbilical cord looked like a hairy arm. I dreamed she
dreamed of crawling back inside, and I yearned to let her go
back in; I breathed myself larger to make a space for her. And
that kind of breathing means something, sure, as smells mean
something when we haven't slept far enough inside ourselves
and walk around all day like a half-opened door. The fragrance
of wild orange blows through our house all night while we
sleep, intoxicating memories.

I opened the back door one late night and walked out
and knew what it would feel like when I had at last to disappear.

*

When doctors cut open this old man to fix his heart,
they found a tree, just behind the breast bone,
thick and leafy, tall, full of insects,
animals, and birds.

And when they dug deeper, they found not just
the one tree, but a whole forest full of flowers,
rivers and animals they'd believed extremely rare,
even extinct. They discovered they could wander
into this forest, just by pulling back
the dead man's chest like a door, ducking,
and stepping in—

Abide with Me (excerpt)

That first year together, we lived in the shadow
of a fishing line factory, next to a super
highway, under a railroad bridge,

behind a field of junked cars—mountains
of tires, hub caps and smashed glass—and we

prayed fervently for our love to return
this world to the poised grace we could imagine
when we touched each other just right, or when we saw sunlight
glint on the stream full of chemicals and junk
that ran by the factory walls.

We prayed with our yearning. That year we could float things
in midair on the hymns
we sang in perfect harmony.

We practiced one hymn—"Abide With Me"—
until we could lift cancered minnows from that stream,
until we could lift stray cats and junkyard dogs,
until we could lift each other as high
as our voices carried. We harmonized versions

of our families and secrets, until we could float
each other in unison, knowing if we fell silent
for even one moment, we'd fall . . .

After Months of Careful Deliberation

my love has decided to take me apart.
She says I've been forgetting things lately; she wants
to see me laid out on the floor so she can tell
what's broken and replace it. My love is good
with her hands; she loves to examine things closely,
to figure out by touching how the world works.
As a child in Colorado, she tied her own flies.
She doesn't mind gutting things, cutting things, mending.
She's an expert with a map. When we drove cross country
in a VW bus, twenty years ago, she had to crawl
between the front tires and hold a connection
every time we started up. I turned the key.
That was the trip we drove to Northern Maine
to visit her old friend in his cabin in the woods.
Snow fell as we drove although it was only
October. That was the trip we got lost
in a blizzard, looking for this old friend
who knew about trees and the way water flows
underground for thousands of years before
we drink it, who'd taught her so many wonderful
facts about nature. And I just followed her,
yearning to see something wild, a moose
or even a bear, wondering where
this great friend was living, hoping we'd never find him.

Modern Dance

He listened to his wife moving around the house
humming as she banged things, as she opened doors,
stepped in and closed them behind her, to emerge
from other rooms, muttering in various languages.
He imagined, as he lay there dozing, that his wife
was painting their windows black, so she could
tell him some difficult secret, so she could
take off her clothes beneath her clothes,
ask for something that way, silently.

Anniversary

for Colleen

The horse in our bedroom
came in with the flowers
we picked this early
morning together.

We noticed it first
when you started to sing.

What's left of our beautiful
daughter, who rode
as the sea rides over
the sea, to another shore?

The horse is too big
for our cramped bedroom.

We will ride out tomorrow,
braid its mane
with flowers, turn it
back to the flowers.

Until then we will mount it
quietly, both of us,
here in this small room,
together.

Loons

One rainy late-summer afternoon in Maine
my father and I took a sauna together
in the woods, by ourselves; then we swam in the cold lake,
too far out for me; my father just kept on
swimming. I followed. There was mist across the water
and I worried that he might disappear, that I might
forget the direction to shore.

Just as I called out I couldn't keep up
and was turning back, we swam up against a huge rock,
almost an island, just beneath the surface.
We pulled ourselves out and surveyed the mist
over the water; we couldn't see the shore
or hear anything but our own bodies.

The rain had stopped. We stood there breathing,
naked, when my father started talking, hesitantly
at first, about loons—their mournful songs,
how rare they'd become, how rarely they allowed
humans to see them. He told me other things
I wish I could remember; then he kissed me
between my shoulder blades, sat down on the edge
of that rock so only his shoulders and head
were above the water—while I stood, a skinny boy,
beside him. Then he pushed off, from that sitting
position, slipped into the water, and swam
to shore with his sure stroke, stopping only once
to gesture to me, to follow.

That night I slept on the screened porch, inside
the exuberant, billion-throated calls of just-born
frogs, the scribble of fireflies, the echo
of owl hoot, silence, and the mournful calls—
way out in the mist—of loons, which kept me
awake for hours, trying to listen
closely enough to understand
what they might mean as they sang across the water
and who I might be in that darkness.

Midsummers: The Sound

Many summers, around mid-July,
when the days were stifling, hazy and still,
the cul-de-sac of harbor we lived beside
filled with thousands of slack-gray, foot-long
fish, *mossbunkers*, chased in by the bigger
open-water blues. The mossbunkers pressed into
the harbor, thrashing against each other
for space, until their thrashing depleted
the water of oxygen; then they gasped
to the surface, twisted in circles, slapped
the water with their tails, turned belly up
and died. The bluefish slashed at them then
until their entrails curled out into the water.

My father would come home from work and take
a swim in that harbor water, even
when it was crowded with suffocating fish.
He'd ignore them or breaststroke-splash them away,
swim out to a moored sail boat, hold on there
a moment to catch his breath, and swim back,
immensely pleased with himself.
Then, dripping, he'd examine his roses in the evening
that was filled with the sounds and stench of thrashing
fish. He'd pick a few ripe tomatoes,
sip his whiskey, check the coals
in the grill, and go inside to get
whatever he was cooking or to put some jazz
on the record player: bebop—Monk or Bud Powell.

I remember fireflies, those nights we sat outside
to eat, the breezes that sometimes cleared
the fishy air so we could smell
whatever was blooming, breathe the green life
of summer. I remember the dull clang of ropes
against aluminum masts, the hourly
chime of church bells, the muffled metallic
roar of the commuter trains a mile
or so away, across the harbor
and town. I tried to imagine those trains,
full of strangers and light, as I lay in my bed
those nights of my childhood when I knew as little

as I do now about anything that matters, when I felt
most deeply my lack of understanding
and so had to make up my life. Sometimes

I woke late and heard my parents thrashing
about the house, mumbling, and I wanted
to understand something, so I got up,
stood at the head of the stairs, and listened,
phosphorescent in the dark—and I saw them in their night selves,
moon-fleshed and primitive. Then I turned back
to bed and tried to think up a story
that could make things make sense, until I fell
asleep again. And I think I slept for years,
as the old stories tell us we do, and I dreamed
lives I must have forgotten by the time
I woke again, tangled up inside
my own body, which was so potent
and well oiled, those days, it seemed capable of taking
any shape it called itself, of becoming anything—

The Philosopher

I once knew an old man who tended his garden
summer afternoons, in pressed shirt and bow tie,
suspenders and straw hat. He talked to the flowers
as he worked, using a different language
for each shape and color—all of them made up,
he said. But effective. There was a turtle
the size of a bucket, who lumbered through the grass
or just stood there chewing while the old man worked.
He visits each summer, he told me. *He's an old*
philosopher. Don't touch him. Just watch. You'll learn something
he's come a great distance to teach us. And look here—
He held up a tiny flower whose long roots dangled down.
Behind him, the hill sloped away into the dark woods
that were full of stone walls and old paths that led
to grottos and hideouts I yearned to explore
even then being bulldozed for mansions.

A Simple Tree

The last time I saw her, my grandmother took me
out to a restaurant, ordered us both
daiquiris, sipped hers discreetly, and started
laughing loudly. She leaned then and whispered
a story she claimed to have just remembered
about my father as a boy, trying on her lipstick
to see if it would make him talk differently, know
larger words—and she laughed even harder
at that memory, until she was almost crying.
The restaurant had a big picture window which looked out
at a well tended lawn and some large oak trees.
My grandmother nodded, still laughing, still crying,
and told me, *that world out there is not*
the real world anymore, though it was still itself
when your father was a boy. I don't know what you'll do
when the angels in those trees blow away and the life
we've planted here withers and dies. I'm glad
I won't see it come. I want to be a tree,
I've wanted that a long time. Just to be a simple tree.
She smiled then, closed her eyes and fell asleep
before she'd even ordered. So I ate alone.

Housekeeping

Sunday mornings we walk around our house
collecting the turtles and frogs that have slipped in
during the week, while we worked too hard
to attend to such ordinary chores

and while we gather them we sing, and while we sing
mourning doves line up on the gardenia bushes outside
and look in at us, and listen. While
we sing, our children sleep deeply, growing
fur and vivid senses

inside their bodies, in some other fragile world
that will vanish as soon as we wake them, which makes it
all the more precious and necessary

and so we sing softly, across their dreaming bodies,
of happiness we haven't ever really known
but want to make possible for them, our children,

at least while they're sleeping, by singing these songs
whose words we make up as we sing, and whose melodies
we compose like the wind composes in the trees,
simply by moving our bodies.

The Point of Touching

One night, long after the children and I had fallen asleep,
my wife lit candles in every room of our house, took off
her clothes, and went outside, naked, to sketch charcoal
impressions of the candle-glowing house full of sleepers and
light she loved. Then she took a scissors and cut a lock of hair
from each of us—me, our children, herself—and buried our
hair at the drip line of our gumbo-limbo tree. She played her
cello then, in our candlelit living room, until dawn yawned at
the windows; then she blew out the candles, came to bed, and
slept like a leaf flowing down stream, and slept like words in
some forgotten language. When she woke, at noon, there was
no one home to talk to, so she never told us anything—except
in the way she touched me anywhere that evening, the way
she kisses me some nights: with a yearning that makes me
stop growing older for a few moments, reverses the direction
of my blood, yes, and makes me glow. And that's the point of
touching, isn't it? To make our bodies real? Things like that
are sometimes closer than the world, closer than our words,
closer even than ourselves. So other nights I stay up beyond
anyone, pacing the sidewalk like the good husband I am,
back and forth, back and forth—until I finally wear away and
vanish, like light itself, like life, or like fragrance from the
drowsy flowers growing butterflies and honeybees, growing
webs and brighter hues around our gumbo-limbo tree.

Moon Flowers

This is the hour when opossum shuffle
up to our back door to poke around

in our garbage and teach their pouched kittens how
to play dead; this is the hour when worms

pull themselves from our apples, to slide
across our counter tops, when foxes

comb each other's tails beneath
the yellow lights in our alley, and snails

take the slow journey
across our front porch;

this is the hour when flowers shaped
like baby's fists or ears open

their faces and sing, in voices only
the lightest of human sleepers can hear.

Selections from
Stationary Wind
Swimmer Dreams

Only Child

My father dressed up as though he were my mother
who dressed up like me, who pretended I was her.
We spent a whole year as each other, to discover
who we really were. I still can't comprehend
how my mother's clothes fit me so well,
or how she, with her full figure, fit into my jeans.

My father wore makeup to understand our world.
Certain words, he said, are disguises, like love
and happiness; others wear costumes
woven of translucent wings, as though they could still fly.

I walked around as a middle-aged woman,
afraid some boy might see through my disguise
and tell the whole school. My mother pretended
she looked just like me, but no one was fooled
for long. Except dad. He kept whispering words
of passion into my disguise, asking me to dance.

Planting the House

This man and his wife, happily married
for over thirty years, planted a garden
down the middle of the mattress of their raft-size bed.
They slept so well amidst the vines and flowers
they let the garden spread across the bedroom floor.
Soon butterflies and bees had arrived,
so the husband put a bird feeder in the tomato patch,
a bird bath on the bench at the foot of their bed.

These old people whose children had lives in distant cities
started making love again, started sleeping deeply,
waking up refreshed, and remembering their dreams.
They decided to plant the whole house in vegetables
and flowers. Soon they'd be able to harvest
their dinners without leaving home.

All their rooms grew fragrant with love and blossoming.
When friends visited, they marveled at the old couple's
energetic happiness, but they couldn't see
the fountain or the swimming hole the wife had installed
where the bath used to be. Neither could their children

or even their grandchildren. The swimming hole reminded
the couple of an underground spring they'd swum
naked in, so long ago it felt like a dream,
a dark cave full of clear water and colorless fish
that nibbled their bodies like kisses as they swam out
to the center in the darkness that was lit by a single
hole in the ceiling, through which sunlight streamed.

Anything I Really Mean

There are so many butterflies, our windshield fogs
even when we're doing errands, and we have to pull over,
get out, and scrape their mucky bodies off

to be certain where we are. There's so much wing-dust
in the air, I mostly sneeze instead of saying
anything I really mean. But listen: One evening

my wife and I walked hand-in-hand to the river
that runs through our town.
We watched mica-colored fish rise to snatch yellow
butterflies from twilight. Smiling, my wife

took off her clothes and waded out into
the river, which spreads out into the bay.

She swayed her arms gently and the yellow butterflies
flew up around her. She called back to me
to join her. Dusk thickened around us.

I leaned on the railing and watched her wade deeper.
I watched her dive in and start her pale swimming.
Her clothes were folded neatly on the wall beside my feet.
I listened to her body splash out into the dark.

The Simple Truth

I met a man in the grocery store checkout line
who told me—out of the blue—he couldn't
recognize himself in the mirror, although
he felt perfectly normal otherwise—responsible,
reasonably content, married twenty years.
Each time he looked in the mirror, he told me
while I unloaded my groceries, he saw
a different person, and he had to touch
his cheeks or speak his own name aloud
while he stared at himself, to ascertain who was
staring back at him. He wanted me to know
how hard it was to shave. He wanted to explain
how, sometimes, when he looked at other men
he thought he saw his own features reflected back at him.
He told me he winked to test what he saw,
to see if that other face winked at the same time
or a moment later, in response. That could be
awkward, obviously. He said he thought he recognized me,
reached out and touched my face, standing there in line,
while the checkout woman scowled and the people lined up
behind us made noises of impatience with their carts.
I stared back hard as though I didn't know him,
but then I gave in, reached out and touched
his face in reassurance, and gazed into his eyes.

Several Ways to Vanish

One summer afternoon my girlfriend asked me
to tighten her belt so her waist would look smaller.

While she sucked in her belly, I pulled tight and fastened,
and when she exhaled, her whole body, which was skinny
and frail, bulged around that tight belt.
When I reached out to unfasten the buckle, she batted
my hand away, playfully: *You'll like me even more.*

A family of foxes lived beneath her parents' house.
In the evening when we sat on the porch and held hands
they yapped and barked softly right beneath our feet.
One evening my girlfriend climbed through the crawlspace
between the floor and the ground to try
to scare them away. She'd grown thinner every day.

I could hear her crawling below us while her father
talked about varnishes and waxes and different kinds
of oil, about lubricants and additives, sealants
and adhesives. He talked about plumbing supplies,
about deck stains and mildew. I watched fireflies
rise from the damp grass into the cloudy sky.

Her mother brought out a plate of warm cookies.
My girlfriend knocked on the floor and called
for a flashlight. *Coming dear,* we sang back in unison,
chewing. Her mother poured another glass of milk.

Singing with My Father

When my father first moved us to the suburbs, he loved
to arrange his 78s on the living room carpet,
early in the morning, while he drank his coffee.
He'd lay them out carefully, leaning close,
scat-singing to the titles.

It was hard to navigate that record-covered floor
without stepping on music he loved, so
I watched from the stairs, and listened to his singing,
which was clear-voiced and elegantly improvised, and I
sang along softly
when I recognized the tune.

Sometimes he heard me, looked up, smiling
and sang a little more loudly, in that quiet house
full of our sleeping family; sometimes,
lost in his memories and music, he didn't
notice me, and I was free to harmonize.

Fruit Trees and Flowers

for Matthew Hettich

That May night, almost midnight, when the doctor caught him,
my son looked at first like a seal-child, head pointed,
dark-furred and sleek, not yet fully human.

I panicked for a moment; then I took my first breath
as a father, and I saw him there, and I knew him. When he nursed,

the room filled with his light—
        and though I tried stubbornly
        not to let the nurses
        carry him away,
to prick and measure his perfect, perfectly
innocent body, they took him anyway.

I've planted fruit trees and flowers in my yard,
key lime and gardenia, hibiscus and muscadine.

They will offer flowers, fragrances and fruits
when their season comes, regardless
of how well I care for them
or anything I do.

The Parents

One morning, my wife and I followed our eight-year-old
daughter along a crowded beach
just far enough behind her that she wasn't aware
we followed, as she walked with her energetic stride,
swinging her arms as though she were singing.

We marveled at her independence, at her
fearlessness; we compared her to other
children we knew, who would never have ventured
so far with such self-confidence.

We were congratulating ourselves on our excellent parenting
skills, laughing proudly at her spirit,
wondering where she was going with such
lively determination, when she stopped

and turned to look back: she was crying, with such
deep heaves she could hardly breathe, desperately
lost. She'd been frantically looking for us
and the place we'd left our towels—she feared
we'd forgotten her, gone home without her.

What could we say, kneeling beside her
in the bright sun—we'd been right there
the whole time, behind her, laughing affectionately
at the way she walked, as she walked

the wrong direction to find us, at the way
she looked from behind as she searched for us,
as she howled in such terror
we thought she was singing?

White Birds

We called her Sweetpea, because she was so sweet
and because it made her smile. I don't know how old she was,
certainly near thirty, though she was baby-fat plump,
and she always smiled shyly, like a little child.

She lived with her parents in a small house on the marsh.
Whenever she saw us exploring the swamps
she'd run down to join us, always barefoot, even
in cold weather, even at high tide when the marsh grass
was almost underwater. She had straight brown hair
cut in bangs across her forehead, and delicate hands.
She'd walk with us, talking quick streams of thought
that seemed unrelated unless you really listened.
I wish I could remember what she told us about wind and tide.
I wish I could recall what she said about the rain.

One afternoon, standing in the rushes,
barefoot as always, in water to her knees,
hem of her dress getting wet, looking up
into the white October sky,
she told us there were birds up there, too high
for us to see, going south. *Higher
than the clouds. White birds. And they might be singing
as they fly.* She told us birds like that always
brought good news when they landed. Then she called out
in a clear, high voice, as though to call those birds down,
make them land here, make us lucky.

It was dusk. We stood still and listened to her singing
and listened to the water in the marsh suck and pull,
until a man crossed the road, an old man, and called her:
Mary Catherine, he whispered to her gently,
darling Mary Catherine, it's time now to come home.

Caesura

Sometimes you must live as though you were grass
in a field of tall grass, as though you swayed
like the other grasses, and made the same soft
whisper they make; sometimes you must live

as though you were happy to be an insect or a tree,
as though you were a river, falling into rivers

falling into sea, as though you were a simple word.
Sometimes you must live as a pause inside a sentence,
as a speck of dark in a star-filled sky,
as a single breath. And then you blink your eyes . . .

I woke up in my bed on an ordinary morning
and knew I wasn't really there. Still, I lay there for a while.
The radio was chattering, but it didn't make a sound
except inside my body, which was already gone.

The trees were full of ashes, that silent form of wind;
the wind was full of trees and grass it couldn't help collecting
as it tried to clutch itself into a solid body,
as it tried to speak. But there was nothing to be said.

Another Life

And once, as a child, I was taken to an underground
    spring, down dark stairs, to a cave lit dimly
by a string of bare light bulbs and a single hole
    in the ceiling, way above, through which sunlight streamed.

When I took off my clothes and dove into that cold
    water to swim out, colorless cave
minnows surrounded me, gently kissing
    my legs and naked body,

and when an afternoon rain started falling
    outside, a shower streamed through the ceiling hole,
straight down into the center of the pool,
    which was otherwise still. I floated on my back

and let that shower scour my face
    and eyes while the minnows kissed my body
and the adults who'd brought me there waited patiently,
    indistinct figures against the dark shore.

Selections from
Flock and Shadow

Forgiveness

We could wade from that island into clear ocean
for hundreds of yards before the water
was even up to our knees.
We could sit there and watch small birds, and vultures
so high they hardly seemed to move.
We could walk out even further, to where the sand dropped off,
where the water was dark and muscular—
We could push ourselves out into that dark deep
full of the ghosts of huge fish we feared
were fished out now, even while we shivered
with the fear of being watched from below.
We could reach a sandbar, almost out of sight.
We could stay out until dusk and swim back through the dark.
Or rain could start to fall, so hard we couldn't hear
each other, or ourselves. And sea birds—gulls and pelicans,
cormorants, terns, anhinga—could float
to that sandbar to wait out the rain. They could be
close enough to touch, all around us. And when the rain
stopped abruptly, they could take off
in a burst, all directions. The water could feel cold
as we swam back, and the surface we swam through
could be fresh enough to drink. And it could smell like flowers.

The Father

Yesterday, my daughter came home
carrying a wing she had fashioned in art class,
as tall as I am—which is not very tall
for a person but huge for a wing. It was built
of wire and wax paper that looked like skin,
and hair she'd cut from her classmates' heads
and glued down. No feathers. *That was one of the rules,*
she told me, *we had to build wings without feathers,*
that strap onto our arms. Then we're supposed to fly,
or pretend to, while our friends imagine real birds
and draw us way up there. And then we'll draw them too.

When I tapped the wing lightly it sounded like a drum.
It's beautiful, I told her. Then I went inside
while she strapped the wing on and started running around
the yard, lopsided for a bird: one wing
only makes a person fall over.
So I helped her build a second wing, but it didn't match,
which was all right by me, since I didn't really want her
flying anyway, at least not without
protection: a parachute, or a net to break her fall.
I helped her fail, though both her wings are beautiful.

Maybe they are beautiful *because* they don't quite match,
I suggested over dinner, unconvinced myself.
She scowled. And then she smiled. Later we went out—
after the dew had fallen—and tried
to lift spiderwebs from the trees without
spoiling their symmetry. *These will staunch a wound*
better than a Band-Aid, or a cotton ball, she said
as dusk fell around us, like fragrance or a breeze.
I wanted to ask her *what wound do you mean,*
as though I might staunch it myself, but she was
holding a web suspended in her hands,
like air, or like nothing, and passing it to me.

Selections from
Like Happiness

Something Else

Suppose, one spring, the birds decided
not to fly north, and the animals
sleeping in the woods decided this year
they'd rather not wake, and turned over instead
for another dream.

Imagine one summer the butterflies decided
to stay in their cocoons, or the caterpillars forgot
to wrap themselves up inside themselves
and simply gorged themselves instead
until their season passed. One day the tide forgot to rise.
This is only one way of speaking for the world.

Suppose the spiders stopped weaving, mosquitoes
forgot how to suck our blood, bees
decided not to pollinate flowers.
Suppose the sea turtles never returned
to the beaches that bore them, to lay their moon-drawn eggs.
Or suppose for a moment the rivers held still
and the leaping salmon held still in midair.

Imagine fire stopped burning things to ash
although it still burned. It was no longer hot.
Of course that couldn't happen. So think of something else.

The Lesson

In that 2nd grade classroom, Mrs. Circle said
each of us carries an ocean inside
bigger than we are, like happiness, and full of
fish that live nowhere else in the world
and tides that are pulled by our heartbeats, and low-tide
sandbars to wade far out in the bright sun.
She taught us we can learn to swim there by jumping
out into the water where the water is still
and shallow, holding our breath and moving
our arms and legs gently, gently—*try*
for yourself, she suggested, and we all closed our eyes
sitting there at our desks, while the snow fell outside
and the radiator whispered. I could hear the clock tick
as we all held our breath and swam without really moving
our bodies, like jellyfish, across the beds
of coral that were filled with many-colored fish
whose names didn't matter, Mrs. Circle said,
as long as you let them come to you—
they are like angels—and nibble the tiny
air bubbles that cling to the hairs along your legs and arms.
Feel how they tickle she said, *take a deep breath,*
dive down underwater as far as you can.
Do you see your shadow down there on the sand,
following your body? That's another form of you,
a kind of memory, swimming down below
your only solid body. Don't forget it. Then she clapped her hands
and we all looked up, happy to be sitting there
with our young teacher in that drafty classroom
in the age of extinction and nuclear bombs
we hadn't been taught about yet.

The Teacher

The water from the salt marsh our dream house was built on
rose through the ground floor one full-moon high tide
and ruined everything, while we children were out roaming
the marshes or the schoolyard, where a girl I had a crush on
had let some boys touch her. That was the year
we'd sneak into the school after everyone else
had gone home, when shadows made even the desks
hold themselves with dignity, as though they were alive.

Once an old teacher whose name we didn't know
was sleeping at her desk, head resting on her papers.
Her door stood open, so my friend stepped in.
I stayed out in the hall and watched as he started
to stroke her gray hair with the tips of his fingers,
as though he were trying to understand something
or comfort her—until she sat up, startled
and blinking, and he whispered it was growing dark outside,
and he told her gently it was time to go home.

She stared at us blankly, then put her head back down.
We watched her sleep until the room went dark,
then walked out into the chilly winter dusk
without speaking, and home to our families.

Awake before Dawn

I opened my grief, the secret life explains,
as though it were a trunk of musty old clothes
I found in someone's attic, fashions my parents'
parents outgrew. I held each piece up
to see if it had been chewed, mildewed or frayed.
I tried to smell the sweat that might linger.
Then I dressed in those clothes—both men's and women's—
and walked around trying to remember other lives,
pretending who I had been had never been quite me.

Another kind of man could turn into a tree
and still be a man, and take pleasure in the wind,
in the water that flows up into his body
and out through his leaves like happiness, refreshing
that wind with its green life, the wind that travels everywhere,
poking its nose into root-crotch and grotto,
calling *who's there, who's there* into the emptiness
and moving off quickly, before anything replies.

The Frogs

He loved frogs, so he spent his afternoons
wading in the tall grass, or standing in the leafy water
where the stream turned. Charmed by their stories
of woods and muck, he practiced singing with them
at dusk at pond's edge, while his mother and father
sat talking, with their cocktails, on the porch. As dark fell
his parents called him, most evenings, for dinner,
but sometimes they let him stay down there until the frogs
were hushed by the cicadas, whose conversations
startled him back to himself. He wandered
up to the house through the tall grass, through the dark,
still singing in his own language. Don't think of him now,
drinking in a city bar, talking to strangers
who ignore him. Don't think of him walking out into
the empty street, slightly drunk. He'll be fine.
Think instead of that walk through the dark wet grass,
the sound of a child's body moving through the grass;
think instead of those frogs falling silent, of that forest,
of mushrooms that push up overnight like elbows
in the moon-drenched mind of the woods.

Howling at the Moon

After my doctor tells me he's pleased
to tell me I haven't been growing old
nearly as quickly as I was
the last time he saw me, although I'm still
aging faster than I should, he smiles
reassuringly and says, *Good news*:
He has new medicines that might carry me
far into the future with no real side effects
I'll be able to notice, after a while:
After you've lost a certain capacity
for what we call "memories" in our haphazard
lexicon, he says. He smiles more broadly
and leans closer with a wink
and a joke: *But it's nothing*
like losing your soul. And of course I have to smile too,
at the mention of *soul*, which he pronounces like *seal*
in his foreign accent—a creature I've always
been fond of, my favorite in the zoos of my childhood.
I loved to watch them swim around their small pools,
so much that when my family set off for the lions
and bears I'd stay put with a handful of pellets
to feed them, laughing at the way they cavorted,
so sleek and cool. One summer afternoon
I saw a boy fall into the seal pool. He bobbed there
laughing nervously while the seals whizzed past,
until a zoo-man threw a rope ladder over the wall
and he climbed up, small hero, to be smacked by his mother,
so hard the popcorn she was holding in her other hand
went flying all over his head, and the crowd
that had gathered around them laughed and clapped
and the pigeons fluttered up into the sky.

By the time my family returned there was only
a puddle on the blacktop to prove my tale was true.
They made skeptical faces and my brother started singing
"Soul Man" as "Seal Man." My mother took a snapshot
of us all smiling there. That was the year
I tried to swim too far underwater and got lost.
That was the year I forgot my other languages,
forgot my sharper senses, slept in my dreams
in the scrubby bushes at the scrappy end of town,
so different from this town, this air-conditioned doctor's
examination room where I sit, shirt off,
strapped to chilly instruments, holding out my hand
for a prescription I will never fill,
at least not until I've tried sweat baths, homeopathy,
herbs and acupuncture, as I did years ago
when the noises of motors and sirens seemed louder
than I could withstand. The old acupuncture healer
stuck me with a single needle in the perfect place,
talked to me in Mandarin, which I understood
as long as the needle was in me, and allowed me
to hear entire symphonies inside my body,
loud enough to drown out every ugly sound:
Everything I looked at had its perfect timbre,
so I could make music by looking at the world.
Alarms and loud trucks, leaf blowers, commercials,
ugly loud guitars could vanish at a blink,
into beauty. So maybe I should track him down now,
old wizard, to slow down my aging; maybe
he could puncture my body to change my story
into a song I could sing again
and again with myself, in harmony, as though
I were a choir—or sing some other animal
somewhere in primeval woods, howling at the moon
until it grows full again, then sing for it to wane
into perfect darkness and its billion-year-old stars.

The Funeral

Today I am walking around our town,
down to the waterfront, up the hill to the small church
that looks out across the harbor, and into the chapel
with its wonderful stained glass windows
and its one clear window with the stunning view

where I sit down a moment to cool off and whisper
a prayer for the small scorned creatures, the ones
no one appreciates, the roaches and termites,
the fire ants and maggots, though I don't much admire
these creatures either and have trouble finding
the appropriate words. So I just sit still

and try to hear the seagulls way down in the harbor,
and listen to the pigeons in the rafters, as I watch
a woman in black shuffle slowly down the aisle.

She leaves a trail of perfume that reminds me of something.
Suddenly I'm trying to remember where we've met,
yearning to make some sort of contact,
though she has her back to me, and she's dressed all in black,
kneeling now, way up front,

as other people enter the chapel, all of them
dressed in mourning, fragrant with that perfume.
So I get up and walk out of the church instead of crying.

Outside it's too bright. Old people are feeding
pigeons in the park; the cafes are crowded.

As I pass *The Fat Baguette*, someone calls
the nickname that defined my childhood, the name
I tried for many years to deny and then forget,
the name no one's called me since high school, and I look up
from the newspaper I've been pretending to read

to see her, the girl I've thought about so often
all these many years, suddenly transformed
into a middle-aged woman, still beautiful,
sitting there alone, standing now and smiling
as she waves, wearing black, which makes her look even

more lovely against the sea of bright
summer colors, the tablecloths and flowers,
the garish tee-shirts of the tourists drinking
pitchers of beer and laughing with raucous
good humor, saluting this most auspicious day—

I approach this stranger I once loved and tell her
that's not my name now, sit down beside her,
order coffee, and ask whose funeral
we're going to, though of course I know the answer.

And she laughs in response—*you mean mine or yours?*—
holds up her cup for a toast to our health,
asks me my new name, how I see myself these days,
and starts to cry softly, like a whisper.

Lunch

Opening a can of soup for lunch,
he felt a cave open in his kitchen, in the air,
and ducked to step in without thinking.
The cave was damp and absolutely dark.
Curious, he walked in deeper, touching
the wall with one hand, holding the other hand
out in front of his body.
Still hungry for lunch, he decided he'd climb out
in a few minutes to warm up that soup,
then realized he couldn't remember exactly
how to turn around, what it meant to *go back*
in this dark, as though the dark itself
had suddenly become all there was, no matter
which direction he traveled.
When he called out for help, his voice was an animal
he couldn't identify, and when he took his hand
from the wall to brush moisture from his face, he couldn't
find the wall again, even when he groped
frantically toward it. And when he stood still
and closed his eyes to think better—or thought he did—
he saw things more clearly than he could with his eyes
open. He saw a man like him
in a kitchen that could have been his, spooning out
soup, humming along with the radio;
then he watched this familiar man step out
into the garden he must have planted,
flowers and fragrant trees that were blossoming
enthusiastically from the heavy rains
that had finally ended. The sun was bright
and the sky was immaculate. He sat in a chair
in the grass and breathed his garden's rich fragrances
and watched the insects and small birds celebrate,
and he ate his soup slowly. He savored each bite.

The Moon

I woke, fully rested, in some other person's life
and unfamiliar body, until I took another breath
and found myself again. This happened every morning
for at least a year, when I was a girl.
She speaks in a rush, starting to cry,
as if tears might somehow convince him to feel
her strange displacement. He smiles reassuringly,
then asks who she'd been then, if she can remember,
and she talks about elk and antelope, mountain
streams that leap into emptiness, snow
doubling itself until everyone is buried.
She tells him her grandmother found her lying
in tall grass with a broken wing, carried her inside,
placed her in a shoebox by the window and fed her.
She flew off in a few days, forever, like a whisper.
She knows, she says, how it feels to be a train
full of cattle, full of people, full of things: I am the schools
of fish inside your body and I am the seaweed,
the tide that holds us. *But the moon pulls that tide,*
he counters, reassuring her. *Let me be that moon—*

Yearning

We had been walking through a field of ferns
in the middle of the forest. We sat down to eat
at their far edge, talking and listening. The day was still.

Beyond us, the river moved unseen.

But we turned back instead, returned through that field
of ferns full of ticks, which jumped off and clung
to our ankles and legs, dug their heads in and sucked us.

Later a pileated woodpecker flashed up
from the undergrowth, across our eyes, up into
the towering sweetgums. And back home, that evening,

we pulled the ticks from our bodies and each other's
bodies, wincing, wondering how
they survive, such creatures, hidden in places

where nothing might venture for months, or a year,
and how they prepare themselves, when they hear us in the distance
finally moving toward them.

Selections from
The Animals Beyond Us

Even Sleeping

I hug my love's body in the warm night in sleep
and we sweat together, while outside some bird
calls out. We hear that song, even
sleeping, and it changes the shape of our dreams.

We both believe in animals no one has named.

Standing in a slow-moving elevator up
a stranger tells me he was swimming just beyond
the waves and sand bars when a huge fish
or even a whale swam by, its body
brushing his legs. Then we step off together

and go our separate ways. Many years ago,
when my children were small, a mockingbird flew
into the elevator I was riding in alone.
It flew against the wall, stunned itself, and fell
to the floor, so I cupped it in my hands and walked

from office to office asking for a window
that would open so I could put it on the sill there
until it came to and could fly. But those windows
don't open, so I carried it outside,
set it gently down in the root-crotch of a tree,

and went back to work. I love the way those birds sing
in other birds' voices and even with the cries
of barking and our human sounds. The truest love is every day,
we understand that now, even sleeping.

The Lake

This girl I hardly knew, taller than I was
and skinny, who made us boys
puff ourselves up and show off how far
we could throw rocks, or how many times
we could skip stones across the choppy water;
this awkward kid I'd never really spoken to
asked me one afternoon to swim across the lake with her.
We were sitting on the dock. It was chilly, but I said
I'd try, though the other side was almost
out of sight, and it would take until dark
to make it there and back. So we dove in and started off
slowly. As we swam, mostly breaststroke, she talked
about the lake, how old it was, what sorts of creatures
lived there now, how it had changed
over its lifetime, the depth of its winter
ice, how the fish huddled on the bottom
between the ice and mud. Then she asked me
what I knew and I had to say, *Nothing much at all.*
Then, despite myself, I made up a story
about the stars; I sang a song
I made up as I sang, about the constellations.
Soon she was singing with me. We'd reached
the middle of the lake, out of breath but singing,
when we realized the other side was too far. We treaded
water there, then turned and headed back, quiet now.
We were tired. We climbed out and walked our separate ways
home through the dusk light, to our families
in silence. No goodbyes. And we never spoke again.

The Bullfrogs

When we first moved to Miami from Vermont
we were so happy to have left the cold
that every time we went into the Everglades, every time
we pulled off the road there, we had to take off
our clothes for a swim in the black water, rejoicing
at the sweet warmth. We'd delight in what we called
the bullfrogs as we swam out, their resonant croaks.
We reveled at the sweet smells and balmy breezes
as we floated on our backs to watch the buzzards circle.
We marveled at the fact that so few people
came out here to swim: The water smelled like flowers.
For that whole first year we had no idea
those croaks we found so charming were actually
challenges from bull alligators establishing their territory,
calling anything in the immediate vicinity
to make love or fight, and they were hungry too.
We just swam out, naked and happy.
Then we got dressed and drove home through the dusk
along a two-lane highway that was littered with the bodies
of car-struck wild animals: vultures and opossums,
turtles, snakes, raccoons. We hardly talked
as we drove, relaxed and clean from our swimming.
Sometimes you looked out the window as the dark fell.
More often you fell asleep beside me.

The Cats

Anyone can learn how to do the things we all do,
but it takes a genius to think like a cat,
especially a stray cat with kittens, who lives
in the gardenia bushes by the front door.
Of course I don't mean a *real* cat, I mean an animal
of the mind. Otherwise it's just ordinary life.
Anyway, the mother cat disappeared, and one of her
kittens starved to death in our front yard.
So we're feeding the other two until we can abandon them
with a clear conscience, when they're big enough
to fend for themselves. In the meantime, we've given them
names we don't mention aloud, for fear
they'll come when we call. But these aren't dogs,
after all, these cats of the mind, small rituals
we live by. They've been trying to slip
into the house when we open any door,
so we pet them as we shoo them, as we go in and out,
until they start to purr, and another kind of silence
rises from their bodies into ours.

Doubles

We loved to pretend that somewhere—on the other side
of the world—were people who looked exactly
like we did, right down to our secret moles and scars.
We imagined them doing just what we did,
thinking exactly what we thought.

Sometimes we imagined we might set up a meeting
between ourselves. What would happen if we did that?
Would we merge? Would one of us have to disappear?
How would our parents react, if they saw us
together? Didn't they have doubles too?

And although we knew it was just a silly game,
still there was something reassuring in discussing
this other who was not someone else exactly,
who actually lived so far away

we knew we'd never meet him. We'd heard all those stories
about animals that turn into uncles and wait
to devour little children, and houses full of wolves
dressed up like grandparents, at the end of long paths
through the woods, or even through an ordinary neighborhood,

and we didn't believe them, most of the time,
either. Our own parents never dressed as wolves
except when we begged them to. Once they made a fire
in the backyard, out of clothes we'd outgrown and snapshots
of people they insisted we didn't recognize.

Uncle James looked like taffy as he melted into flames.
Aunt Betty seemed to grow a beard, and then she was just ash.

The Halo of Bees

The jasmine is flowering with so many bees
I thought for a moment some motor was caught
in its branches, as its fragrance woke me
to a vividness usually available only
to those who can still themselves, and listen to their blood
coursing through their bodies as if
their bodies were not them at all, but merely
the necessary vehicle, the structure that holds
the world intact. Each blossom held a bee
which buzzed until nightfall. And what if I'd stood there
while a thunderstorm pelted those blossoms to the ground?

There are old men huddled under cardboard, just outside
our neighborhood; there are barefoot women
singing as they walk through pelting rain
just before morning. And of course there are the children.

House of Light

Someone breaks open like a seedpod or a flower
to spill out across the street, and we all keep walking by
because it is too beautiful to notice, or too frightening,
as the river just moves on, the clothed and dreaming river,
the speaking river feeling just the way it needs to, nothing more.
There are feathers in the sky. Say *birds*, generic things,
or simply ignore them. But what about those other people
bursting into flame? Will they singe you? Step away
from those other fires, as though you weren't wild yourself
in all the parts that matter: in your blood and vivid thinking, seeing
colors for their secrets: how to move and be and feel
until you burst aflame. Some buildings built of stone are made
to echo now and then, forever—no one can escape—
but others made of wood are filled with window after window,
so many windows you could never open all of them
in a single lifetime. No one lives that long. But you could open some.

The Seamless World

Driving to work, I saw a black snake
in the road, the back of its long body
flattened into the street by a car,
its front still trying to slither away
as though nothing had happened, as though it thought
it might start moving any moment now, off into
the grass, while traffic passed close; it was obvious
soon enough another car would crush it.

Look at the stray dogs when they try to cross a busy street;
watch the way they stand there trying not to look
undignified, waiting for the traffic to break.
Sometimes they start across anyway, in the way
my own brother started off one winter afternoon
after he'd been sick for a long time, still a puppy—
just hurled himself out across our living room
from the shore of one couch to another.

This Burning

I tried to do the same things every day for a week
without thinking about it, as though I could layer
myself across myself. Why not? It's just a version
of how it all happens anyway, in the now
that everything inhabits. This is a kind of weaving
or like building a stone wall without stones, and living
back there in the space made coherent by its border.
I moved through the days without variation.
I said the same things to the same people
who must have been moving the same ways themselves.
We did this until we had worn ourselves clean,
and then I think we vanished—although I'm not certain,
as I seem to be here with myself right now.
Even in your memories you are growing old.
Your thoughts are emerging fully formed from your head.
If a man's hands started suddenly burning, would you let him
embrace you? Your clothes would burst alive with flame,
all the downy hair along your arms and legs,
your eyebrows and eyelids. And your private silences,
whatever they are now, would start burning too
as though they were made of some substance, something real
and necessary. Listen to me: All your nights and days.

Widow

If silence were a creature like a dog, and could follow you
around like a dog does, and come when you call.
If silence were a housecat you rescued from the alley,
pampered and declawed, who sits and purrs, ignoring you.
If silence were the small birds who come to the suet
you've hung outside your kitchen window,
who bang themselves sometimes against the glass
and tumble to the sidewalk. If silence were the journey
you take down the stairs to revive them, breathing
into their delicate faces like a song.
If silence were the way they leap up and fly away,
headed, you imagine, for more exotic climes
where the trees are brighter and the flowers intoxicate
in ways they just can't where it's cold. When it's cold
you love to walk out, until you're lost, like snow.
When it's cold you make fires in your hair and in your clothes
which you think of as ghosts, or lovers.
When it's cold you understand things by leaving them alone.
Taste me, the cheese and apples on your plate
seem to whisper while you look out the window at the birds,
winter birds gorging themselves on your suet
while you sit burning inside.

Skin

Some people can watch other people turn to air
without thinking the air becomes wind too, so it can fly.
I have been like that, capable of watching
as a leaf does, or a window: When she ripped off her skin,
my mother, and lost herself standing there before us
without any skin, and insisted she'd be fine.
When we gathered her shed skin but wouldn't slip it on,
not even over our clothes: It was lumpy
and covered in varicose veins she'd gotten
from the weight of our bodies inside hers, years ago.
When we put her to bed without her skin and turned off
the night light and told her to sleep as long
as she wanted to, forever if she wanted to; we would make
breakfast in the morning. When we sat in the kitchen
and looked at each other
and talked about her skin.

The Winds

And so they collected those skittish winds that blow
between darkness and first light, lassoed whatever
allowed the wind to move, they tied it with a slipknot—

and the wind stood there waiting like a tree or a house;
it didn't try to struggle; it just stood there as other winds
began to grow restless, winds that usually

slept until daylight, winds that slip down
before rain, winds we call Son-and-Daughter, Memory,
and send off to school like some failure of imagination

to see how they will do there, who else they might become.
And when they'd collected enough wind for everyone,
after many mornings of austerity and work,

they dug holes to plant the wind—or tried to—in the fields
where their ancestors were buried; some of those winds
understood what was required and stood perfectly still

until they were the farmland and orchards that make
this region so fertile. But others, their brothers
and sisters, were not so docile: After all, they whispered,

these people had trapped them and tied them in bundles
without the least concern for their pride, or for their fragile bones—
and so they decided to seem human for a while

until they could blow things apart from within.
They started to move like nothing with a vengeance,
driving cars and building houses: *On, and on, and on.*

The Small Birds

They ask us to understand our grief
by simply leaping out, trusting the air
which is far more complex than sorrow, to follow
all we've ever done with a pure heart and change
completely, but never for long.

Someday, you say, you'll be glass in a window
that looks across a landscape of wilderness and snow
which will melt when you go out there, because
you've loved someone well. But whom do you love,

after all? For now, you open that window
and lean out. For now you just watch things: vivid rugs
on hardwood floors, closets full of clothes
that would never fit you, where another person's smell
lingers for years. And then it vanishes.

Selections from
The Measured Breathing
Systems of Vanishing

The Ancestors

watch us from behind the scree
and trifles of our lives. *You think you're alone
in your moment?* they ask—the way a leaf shivers
without breeze, or a breath is inhaled
where there is no body. We call it *the wind*
while the ancestors watch us like the dark inside daylight
makes the wild animals move through the trees
until we can't see them. Until they have no names.
You might call them birds, but the ancestors are never birds.
Maybe stones or grasses. Wildflowers. Forgotten words.
—Now someone whispers, *the wild birds are going
extinct, the warblers and thrushes that migrate
thousands of miles.* Or the way summer fragrances
cover the scent of things falling back to earth
as the ancestors did long ago, living here
in breath and marl and swelling fruit although
we refuse to acknowledge them, as we pretend
our muscles, senses and hearts are our own
and everything lives only now.

The Old Friend

calls to tell me he can't see the same things
he saw yesterday; the book he was reading
last night has become an album of photographs
of his wife's family back in the old country—
people he's never even met—and his wife
herself has been replaced by the first girl he ever
asked on a date.
                              He tells me it snowed
so hard that night, they'd made a snowman
instead of going to a movie. He says
he'd stood still and let the snow cover him
while she made angels. Now his hands won't move
the way they used to, and his voice speaks as though
someone else were standing behind him, like
a puppeteer, someone not like him at all.
What am I to do? he asks.
                              *Sing the songs
you love most,* I tell him. *And wait for me,
I'm on my way.*
                              But when I get there,
he's not in his house or garden, though his car
is sitting out front as usual; his wife
is puttering in the rose bushes, singing to the boom box
set on the back porch, which churns out golden oldies.
Where has he gone? I ask her. And she looks up,
confused expression on her face, smiles
sweetly and whispers, *Whom do you mean, my love?*

The Jam

So one day he woke up, opened his closet
to get dressed and found all his clothes hanging
in tatters, falling to the floor as dust.
All the towels in the bathroom looked like spiderwebs.
His wife was sleeping peacefully at last, after days
of fret and obligation. He didn't want to wake her
and he didn't want to stay home from the office, but
he was naked. What else could he do? And so
he picked up the guitar he hadn't touched in months,
sat down on the wood floor and strummed like he used to
in the old days. He woke her after all,
who lay there a few moments remembering when he'd
sung like a young man. Then she got up, opened
her closet to find all her clothes tattered too.
Her husband was howling now. What could she do
but slide her old cello out from under the bed?
And so they jammed for hours. Then they lay back down
exhausted—it was afternoon already—
and slept, and dreamed vividly. And when they woke up
refreshed for the first time in months, laughing
at their predicament, they found their closets
replenished with stylish new garments, sharp suits
and elegant skirts, freshly pressed and perfumed.
Astonished at their luck, they tried on these new clothes
but found that none fit, not even close. This could go on
for a long time they realized as they undressed again
with a kind of glee and giggling, until
they realized their bodies had grown unfamiliar,
thicker than they used to be, calloused where they used to be
pink with small veins scribbled everywhere, and nerves
that had danced at the slightest provocation
and had now moved far off to some hideout in the distance
that would take at least a day to hike to, climbing
rocky terrain over poorly marked trails,
naked and numbed from this hunger.

Nectar

I was dozing in a hammock on a gorgeous afternoon,
    dreaming I was doing what I was doing,
knowing I'd forget my dream when I woke,
    and sensing I'd wake soon. Small birds kept landing

on my body, sweet birds no larger than my thumb,
    yellow and blue birds, black birds trimmed with rust.
They smelled like baby powder without the dust,
    or jasmine at dusk. Each took something from me

as I dozed: first the buttons of my shirt, one after
    the other; then the ring my wife had given me;
the pens in my shirt pocket, then the shirt itself—
    they took the loose threads in their beaks and flew up

into the trees. And when they'd unraveled
    my clothes they started pecking at me, so gently
I didn't wake, and I didn't wake when my wife came out
    and found me, just a head without ears by then

and only half my body lying there, still asleep.
    She spent the rest of the afternoon searching
for the parts of me up in the trees, putting me
    back together while I slept, so I'd never notice.

Then she lay down beside me in that hammock, and slept
    until I woke and hugged her. I blessed my good luck,
hardly knowing the least of it, and listened to the birds,
    the hummingbirds buzzing through the late afternoon,
searching, as always, for nectar.

First Day of Class

I was thinking of starting a forest, he says
when I ask what he plans to do with his life
after he graduates. *If I did that,*
he explains, *I would have to learn self-reliance
and I'd understand the animals. I wonder how many
trees I'd have to grow to become
a forest, a real one.* The other students listen silently
and some even nod, as if what he said
were something they'd considered too. But they've all told me
lawyer or *physical therapist, nurse*
or *businessperson.* There have been no dancers
or even English majors. But this young man is serious,
sitting there in tee shirt and baseball cap, straight-backed
and speaking with a deferential nod, as though
I could help him—as I've been explaining I'm here
to do, their professor. We'll form a small community
I've told them, or I hope we will, and we'll discuss the world.
It seems to be raining this morning, though I'm not sure
since this classroom doesn't have windows. It was raining
when I drove in at first light, splashing through the streets:
Some of the students wear slickers; others carry
brightly colored umbrellas. And now another young man
raises his hand and says that, on second thought,
he wants to be a farm, an organic farm with many bees
and maybe even cows and pigs no one will ever eat
that live like pets. *I love fresh milk,* he says.
Then someone else tells us she's always secretly
yearned to be a lake somewhere up north in the woods—
*let's say in Maine, since I love seasons
and I wonder how it feels to freeze tight, not move
for months, how it feels to open up again
in the spring; and I've always wondered how fish would feel
swimming through my body, how that might make me shiver
like love.* She laughs then. And thus the room grows wild.

Daughter in the Sky

That story of a ladder found propped against the air
by a young man out walking one brisk afternoon
to clear his fuzzy head; that story of his looking up
and shaking the ladder, of climbing up a little;

the story of him telling his family what he'd found;
the story of him leading his family to that ladder—
daughter holding mother's hand, son held tight
in the young man's arms—the story of their climbing

so slowly it took all the light from the day
to get there, the little girl crying until
she found herself amazed, yearning to climb
even higher, by herself, when her parents stopped

and stepped off into a landscape of silence
to look up at the stars and their daughter, still climbing.
The story that develops, at this point, in a whole new
direction—of how that ladder fell,

which is mostly the story of the daughter, way up
against the sky, who was still just a baby,
really, although she'd learned many languages
already, whose parents spoke mostly as grass

or wind-in-the-trees now and didn't even seem
to remember her at all, though she called out, climbing
through the constellations and off across the dark
where no one could find her, forever.

Certain Constellations

. . . of a silence so vast all sounds have meaning.
—Lisel Mueller

Our star fruit tree, *averrhoa carambola*,
   produces at least three crops each year,
      so many succulent fruits with each harvest
that over half of the fragrant, flower-shaped,
   delicate-tasting delights rot
      in the grass, despite our best intentions
to pick and eat or give them all away.
   The tree is just too generous, though
      we do nothing for it. In fact we pay it
little attention, as we putter
   in the garden, breathing its perfumed shade.

   But imagine if we simply let the fruit lie
and rot where it fell in the grass: soon
   a small forest of *carambola* trees
      would spring up and start moving across our backyard,
each sapling spreading saplings as far
   as its branches extended, a slow motion migration.

   Imagine the bees and birds, the feasting
rodents and raccoons, the insects. Such fecundity
   boggles the mind, if you really think about it,
      which I don't, or not often—or not often enough,
even as I cut and savor a slice
   of sweet *carambola*, or pass it to my wife
      and guests, as we sit here in the evening with a glass
of wine, talking movies, and politics, and friends
   we haven't seen in years, of friends we'll never see again—

   And soon we are telling these friends about the cabin
we stayed in at Christmas, about the hunters and skeletons
   we found in the woods there, about the deer and alligator
      bones we gathered and took home—they're inside
the house now, waiting to be fashioned into something
   by our daughter, a sculptor—and we talk then of backpacking
      in the wilderness a little bit deeper in those woods,

as ambient music our son gave us whispers
    from the kitchen where the vegetables, cut up and skewered
        and ready to be grilled, soak up their olive oil
and just-picked basil, and a jet groans across the sky,
    heading east, toward the islands.

                                        This morning
a student came by to show me his new
    poems imitating the writers I'd suggested
        he read the last time I saw him—yesterday—
and he happened to mention in passing, that since
    he has no electricity in his house—his mother's
        lost her job—he was staying with a friend,
on his couch, and when I asked him how
    that was he said "fine," just "fine," and shrugged
        dismissively. He just wanted me to look at

his teeming new poems, which were about everything
    he could think of and some things he was feeling, mostly
        love for a girl he'd known in high school,
who'd moved away now, to college. As always,
    he asked me who to read now, thanked me, and shook
        my hand as he left. *He's the real thing,* I say,

as we feel the evening settle down
    around us, as we look up to see
        if there are any stars—which reminds Colleen
of a man we met this summer at Chaco
    Canyon, on the evening of the solstice, a naked-eye
        astronomer with a telescope he'd carried from Colorado,
who would talk to anyone willing to listen,
    about constellations, their names and the myths
        they'd represented in Ancient Greece
and the Far East, in various Native American
    and European cultures—and the current scientific
        designations of each star in the pattern.

He knew their distance, how fast they're moving.
   Everywhere we pointed up into the teeming
      sky was a story and another story. Next morning,
the solstice, we got up before dawn to watch
   the sun rise at the central *kiva*: First light
      would shoot through a chink in one wall, to land
in an indentation carved into
   the far wall, then move across that wall, precisely
      as it had done at every solstice
since that *kiva* was built, 1000 years ago.

   At the site, the astronomer prayed silently,
      off by himself. All around us the ground
         seemed to glitter, and if we had walked along
the canyon we would have been able to study
   the petroglyphs etched across those walls
      gleaming in the first light.

                                        Are we ready
for the food? Colleen asks now, lighting a candle,
   as the music from inside the house dies away
      for a moment and we hear something singing from the firecracker
bushes across the garden, a creature
   none of us has heard before, a gentle warbling-
      coo that sounds like any mother-mammal
watching her baby sleep, and we all

   get up quietly, pushing our chairs back
      slowly, slowly, so as not to make a sound
as we tiptoe across the grass, careful
   not to disturb whatever's been singing,

      so we might move into
      the circle of its song.

                              for Jesse Millner

119

The Problem of Analysis

This city is so large, no one could possibly
walk every street in one lifetime, even
walking every day. In fact, this city
has grown so massive it might not even *be*
a city, properly speaking, but more like
the nerves and atoms in an ordinary brain
of someone who happens to be sleeping, let's say—

and if we could sneak inside her as she dreams,
stilling our breath not to wake her, we might
look more closely up and down the meandering
alleys, peer along the hallways and alcoves
of the buildings inside her, of the lives there—as now,
through a half-opened window on the second floor
a young man sits reading. When his phone rings,
he answers, distracted, looking down
at the street, where a beautiful woman is walking
a dachshund who poops in the middle of the sidewalk
while she pretends to examine her manicure,

which infuriates the young man, who tosses his phone
and leaps through the door to the street, to give her
a piece of his mind—which makes this a good time
to move in deeper, into another neighborhood,
where an old man who looks like a dog in a bathrobe
is pouring milk into a fish tank
crowded with pollywogs, or to a public swimming pool
where children are engaged in a race to see
how fast they can drink all its water. At the bottom

something is moving. And one boy, a show-off,
keeps jumping from the diving board, trying to swim
to the bottom and touch that shape—whatever
it is—before it lies still. On another street,
trains full of feathers fly past waiting rooms;
someone gathers spiderwebs to make a violin
while caves are being dug in the ground behind the bleachers
by girls who were cheerleaders before they grew moss;

and still we move deeper, stealthily, growing
harder to see as it grows harder
to see ourselves anywhere, until we can't help

becoming more like the trees and birds
that sang here a thousand years ago than we are
like ourselves, dear city of the inner life,
until we are less than a smidgen of sap
that might once have quickened a now-extinct species
of flower that smelled like the sky, deep
in the layers and folds of our memories, where

we're nothing like ourselves, where bees still gather
pollen with a buzzing that fills the afternoon
wherever that afternoon *is*, and pollinate
other long-extinct flowers to make
honey as sweet as this brief time we've been given

to breathe.

The Colorblind Man

I walked through a parking lot full of black birds
as I headed to the beach for a swim. Black birds
were floating in the waves, just beyond the breakers
where the water gets deep. There was no one else
at the beach, so I took off my suit and swam naked.

The black birds flew up as I swam out. There were other birds
in the sky, almost out of sight, circling. They were black too.

My body felt pale in the cool water, which was clogged
with seaweed filled with small eels; they tickled
as night fell. Bodies started moving through the water,
brushing my legs and making me sing.
No one could hear me. The bodies bumped up

against my nakedness as though we'd been friends once,
long ago, and the black birds started landing
on the beach, huge flocks that huddled up and fell asleep
as the night grew more solid around us.

Dust Train

She tells me about the Greeks, who believed the past
was before them, and the future behind, because the
past they could see, but the future was hidden, always
out of sight.
                                    —Gary Young

1.

On the last healthy day of our lives we'll dream
        backward, she insisted, and unravel our memories
like a spun top growing smaller, back to the moment
           we were born, back to the moment we were

mere potential, when our parents made love,
        back even farther, before they even touched,
back when desire first awakened and the mystery
           trembled between them. *We call this the birthplace*

of the soul, she told me, *and as we leave this life,*
        we return there, like a cloud might return to rain.
She claimed that other cultures, cultures she preferred,
           taught children to carry honey bees in their mouths

which buzzed through the winter, so when they kissed
        something else happened. Their silence was not
the same as our own; then she claimed we could eat
           the gestures we'd try to protect ourselves with

if we were really starving. But we're not, so we hardly
        live except by artifact, or someone else's story.
This is why hair grows all over our bodies
           in all its tiny follicles, and why it fills with dust

or dusk when the weather is just right, and the windows
        glint in the sunset that was once filled with birds
flying in small flocks just overhead
           back to their rookeries, beyond this empty sky.

2.

A person put together like a bundle of sticks, tied tight with
twine and leaned in a corner because he or she looks beautiful
there. A person swept up like sawdust on the shop floor after
a day spent building sturdy furniture. Or a person imagined
in the egg-filled nest abandoned in the live oak, a nest that
will fall in the wind. I told you one morning a person was an
empty train moving through the mountains at night and waking
a woman who listens to the wind in the trees when the train
passes. Then she gets up and goes outside in her nightgown,
walks across the chilly grass and steps into the creek that runs
across her property. She stands there feeling the cold water and
the stones. Then she returns to her house and lies back down.
Her skin is the color of a candle in the dark.

And you whom I've loved forever disagreed, asserting that a
person is something else entirely, a subway car full of sweating
strangers, rushing under the river at night while tugboats and
tankers negotiate the currents and flounders look up from the
mud. A person is the newspaper an old man crumples and
throws to the floor, to be kicked around by all those aching
subway feet, and a person is the woman who leans to pick it
up, smooths it meticulously and begins to read.

She will walk home soon through the balmy summer streets, to
her husband who's cooking and singing as he waits for her. A
person is the sidewalk that leads to her front stoop. A person
is the music she hears in the distance, a song she remembers
from church. She hums it, growing hungry as she walks. A
person, I said then, is the glass of wine she'll savor, the toast
she'll share with her husband. But another kind of person is the
bike someone stole from the rack in front of the library, a bike
which was given in love, for Christmas, that's being stripped
now and spray painted gold. On other days a person is more

like the opossum with a baby in her pouch, who sniffs at the
back door. We watch her push the garbage can around, trying
to knock it over but afraid she'll hurt her baby if the can falls
on her, so she gives up and walks off across the weedy grass
to look for papaya, broken open and rotting, for mango or
starfruit waiting in the bushes. A person is that appetite for
sweetness in the dark.

3.

My other Michael barks at night when lizards cross our bedroom floor.
He wakes me up confused, full of needles and needing
to lock the door against the buzzing flies and bees,
against the ravenous mosquitoes. My other Michael

snuggles up against my wife. He breathes into her ear
until the breath he exhales there goes into her so far
it finds itself outside on a cool night full of stars,
this breath we call my other Michael, my better Michael, my Michael

without the drag and half-lies that make things only seem to happen
and allowing him to move. I am moving. My other Michael thanks me
for moving. My Michael, filled with oil and silence.
My Michael, weighed down with dirt and ordinary stones.

4.

These trees that are netted with tightly-woven spiderwebs.
These houses that are knee deep in flowers.
This rain that leaps up when it hits the parched ground
and turns into many small angels. The cold
pavement as the rain falls; the puddles that try
to pretend for their brief lives they're ponds, full of minnows.
The tiny fish that live there until those puddles dry.

The worms that swim underground, a slow-motion cabaret.

The leaves that still drip hours later in the blue day.
The stones that have lived here
since the earth was made.

The grass—you know grass—that is always alive
even under snow. The underground rivers
as powerful as any on the surface, in their darkness.

Above that darkness, in the houses where we live

we are moving through our rooms, as always, in a kind of daze,
as though the whole world wasn't burning.

The Garden

If you could be a feather in a raven's black wing
as the raven caws its mind from a tree
filled with other ravens. If you knew the feeling
of wind through that wing. If you could be the beak
of that raven, or the raven's eye, if you could be
the way the raven—any raven—thinks, if you could be that
thought and still be who you are now, sitting
in an easy chair reading. If you could be a whole flock
of ravens ripping the swollen carcass of a deer
far from any town. If you could be the blackness
of a raven at night. But your book has nothing
to do with birds or darkness; it's a novel
about travel and love you suspect you've read
before, more than once. Outside, the caterpillars
and brightly colored worms are feasting on your lemon tree.
They eat the new leaves to the nub, then fold themselves
tight and sleep. And you will hope to watch them
emerge as butterflies, as though the world were still intact,
which perhaps it is. The way you are reading
makes a kind of closet: there are snakes out there too,
in the garden, black snakes that can feel you move
through the air you both breathe. They feel you as an animal.
You might learn to think like the garden instead,
through which all those breezes are running.

In Winter

Sometimes we saw shadows of gods
in the trees; silenced, we went on.
　　　　　—Galway Kinnell

The old man in the alley behind my house
is singing in a language I don't recognize
as I step out to examine our garden's flowering
mango tree, thinking of friends
in cold winter climates, and imagining the taste
of the papaya ripening above me, of the star fruit
filling the morning with its perfume—the bounty
of my backyard—only half listening
to this old man's strange keening as he shuffles through perfectly
good things our pampered neighbors have discarded:
toys and boom boxes, furniture and books—
too much precious junk for one old man to carry.

In this morning's paper I read, just now,
that the vast ruins of a Buddhist monastery
built two thousand years ago
in central Afghanistan, which sits on one
of the largest copper deposits in the world,
will be pulled down to mine that copper, to make
wire and electronic gadgets, destroying
the ancient statues and temples, most of them
one-of-a-kind, transforming the site
into an open pit, a scab even worse
than was left when the towering Buddhas of Bamiyan
were dynamited by the Taliban. Every day

so much is lost—animals, plants,
whole cultures, languages—and memories, perhaps,
of the older forms of feeling. But now
this old man leans across my fence,
gestures for me to come over; he's smiling
as he holds out a photograph he's found in someone's
trash: a young girl in a fine dress,
smiling at the camera, a black and white portrait
taken many years ago
by the looks of her ruffled outfit and hair.

She's smiling, crook-mouthed and wry, with a haunting
beauty; we stand looking at her silently,
in our separate languages, until the old man
turns away, walks over to my neighbor's junk pile
and places the picture gently there,
turns back to me with a shrug, then continues
down the alley. Of course when he's walked
out of sight, I retrieve that young girl's picture,
bring it inside and tack it on the wall
of my study, so I can watch her, and imagine
her young life, years ago, totally vanished
I think now, except for this picture—though maybe
she's still alive somewhere, old woman listening
to mockingbirds and mourning doves singing outside
her bedroom window, as those birds are singing
now from the paradise trees in my garden.

She dozes and wakes, as she slowly slips away,
even as I look at her smiling down at me
as a beautiful girl smiled once for the camera,
then turned back, without a thought, to her life.

The Measured Breathing

And so I understand, at least for a moment,
how something and nothing can sometimes be reversed,
as I understand nothing: The black in a crow's wing
works like my own deepest sleep when I wake
beyond mere self, that black like the waves
lifting their shoulders in a sudden swell of memory
or just a sudden swell. If everything we needed
were real, those delicate yellow-bellied birds
might fly through this thicket without brushing anything
and I might come home to a house full of absence
and meet all the people I've loved, sitting there
in the bodies they had then, but stuffed now with straw,
propped up and grinning. As my body too
is stuffed with dry grass, which pokes through my clothes.
I was hungry and you fed me—just enough to survive
until I was only what I am now, disappeared
into the music behind all this sound,
as the trees are connected to the trees of their past
through roots and branches and leaves—without thinking
anything we'd ever recognize as thinking,
anything we'd recognize: a place beyond this air.

And We Were Nearly Children

1.

Reading in my garden on a Sunday afternoon,
I realize with a shock that blurs my eyes
when I look up at the flowering bushes and trees,

it's been over thirty years since you died, daughter
I never really knew—as your mother did—beyond
feeling you kick
and laughing, planning
our future together, as your mother giggled

to tell me you were dancing inside her, as she
sewed your baby clothes and imagined

a life you never lived, a life
we never lived, so long past now

I rarely think of you, stunned, as I'm stunned now,
to stare off into space
and remember those days

in Vermont, that beautiful summer of swimming
naked in the crisp West River that ran
along the edge of our town, of walking
the ridge just across
the Connecticut River,
in New Hampshire, marveling at our luck to have found
this place, so richly beautiful. We'd started

a gallery and tiny small press bookstore
and thought we might even make a go of it that way,

so your mother could give you her days, Audrey,
nursing you whenever you desired, carrying you
everywhere, even to the top of Rattlesnake
Ridge, we imagined, to look out over

the valley. And everything went well at first,
even the process of finding a midwife:

She was English, and though
she seemed a bit fierce
and sarcastic to us both, she'd been highly recommended,

so we overlooked our shared intuition
and enrolled in her home-birth training class,
upstairs in her barn those long summer evenings,
with a few other couples; we practiced breathing

and pushing, and we talked about the sadness of hospital
births, the industrial, commercialized loss
of the wondrous experience we were preparing for.

Outside, in the tall grass by the apple trees, there were
fireflies rising, and the stars were thick,
heavy and almost wet with their gleaming.

We were sure of our choice, though our families and some
of our friends were trying to get us to re-
consider home birth: *things can happen* they told us.

                              Of course we didn't listen.

After all, hadn't mothers birthed their children at home
for many thousands of years, and wasn't
that peace and quiet, that quality of *home*
what a newborn needed, rather than needles,
bright lights and prodding? We were sure we were doing

the right thing. Our midwife was well-trained and self-
assured, and we liked her assistant, whose name
I can't remember, who had been our main coach
and who'd probably be there at the birth too, so were weren't

worried. We thought about names. We were excited

*

and well prepared. We'd asked a friend
to help with the birth, and we'd stocked up on towels
and ice, juices and tea. We

had Steve Reich's *Music for 18 Musicians*
all ready to play, as we waited for the big day
to come. It was fall. I'd started working

at a start-up magazine, *Family Journal*, out
in the country, in a farmhouse. I worked side-by-side
with the owner-editor, surrounded by his wife

and children, who bustled in and out of the cramped room
we worked in while he gave me numbers to cold call:

toy companies, food companies, well-known magazines

and somehow convince them to advertise with us,
a job I was totally unsuited for, made
impossible by the dead rat or squirrel under
the house, that stank so badly we could hardly

breathe. And this editor corrected me constantly
as I made my lame pitch, he wanted me to be
more pushy. I hated everything about it,

except for my lunch break, when I wandered those dirt roads
through apple orchards, planning the life
we'd make here, dreaming of the house we'd find
on a beautiful piece of land by a stream,
someday soon.

                              On the day you were born
and died, Audrey, your mother had gone

out to the country to visit a woman
whose collection of photographs she thought we might show
in our gallery.
                              She told me she'd been walking along

the road there, amidst the swirl of autumn
leaves when her water broke. I remember nothing else
about that afternoon. I remember the evening

*

and the news that the midwife who'd coached us, the gentle
woman we'd liked, had been called unexpectedly
to Maine, so the English midwife attended,

with her own infant daughter sleeping in a basket
beside her. I remember her knitting while we drank tea,

and I remember her distraction, but we were focused
on your mother's breathing, our breathing, on the imminent

birth of *you*, our first child, who'd been
so lively lately, kicking and dancing

inside. We lit candles and dimmed the room,
and the midwife checked your mother now

and then, without saying much of anything
at all—at least that's how I remember it

now. At some point she grew alarmed

*

and we moved from the comfortable chair in the front room
to the mattress on the floor in our bedroom and she told your

mother to push, which she'd been doing,
and she told your mom to push harder, she was leaning

down over your mother growing more
and more alarmed—and the music played on,

and the candles flickered and she started raising
her voice at your mother and ordering me

to do this and that—I obeyed like some sort of
stunned automaton, not understanding

exactly what was going on. Your mother was panting
and pushing and I was pushing on your mother

from behind, pushing hard enough to hurt her;
everyone was bent down and hurting your mother

and hurting your mother who was panting, not crying
but hurt and when the midwife cut

your mother, desperate to get you out, Audrey,
she cut her with a serrated knife, she cut deep

into your mom who was bleeding, even dying—
I'm not exaggerating—and when you slid out of her—

better say when you were yanked out, you were
limp but alive and someone had called

the police who were there then, lumbering presences
in the dim light, with hats and flashlights,

and they took you, our daughter, to the hospital, less
than a mile away, and I stayed with your mom

while the midwife stitched her, brutally and without
anesthetic and your mom cried out, not

for herself. She loved you as a darling daughter,
Audrey, let me tell you now

from the distance of all these years, as fiercely
as any mother could, she wanted only

the best for you. I was there too
and I loved you but not the way your mother did. I loved

your mother and I loved the way she loved you,
and so I loved you, as a father does. And I

missed you; I already missed the life
we never had. And when the hospital

*

called to tell us you were alive,
probably brain damaged from oxygen deprivation,

that you'd never live a full life, probably
survive just a few days, we told them to let you
go

                          and then we went to the hospital

to see you, our dear daughter Audrey, in the autumn
dawn-light and chill; we were shown to a small
sterilized, brightly-lit room where you lay
on a counter, on your back, a perfectly beautiful
girl, our daughter, with blond hair and perfect
hands and feet, perfect fingernails. They were kind to us
there—and they were furious too,

at the loss, *our* loss, but also at the simple
awesome negligence. But that's another story

*

and what I want to say now, Audrey, is that after
you were cremated we carried your ashes
to a bend in the river we'd swum in that summer

when you were so large in your mom, when she was
so proud of you in there she proudly strutted
and held her belly out for all the world to see

and her bright blue eyes twinkled happily because of you;
Audrey, we scattered your ashes beside
that river. And every time we drove

or walked by, we thought of you there, and when
it was cold out your mom would worry you'd be cold
there by the river, and she'd cry that there was

nothing she could do to warm you, and she was
still badly wounded where the midwife had cut her.
We grieved together, and she suffered from her wound

*

which is with her even now, despite the beautiful
children we've raised together.
                                    That winter

your mom took a job as a crossing guard, walking
children back and forth across the busy street
in the morning, at noon, and in the afternoon,

while I drove a bread truck through the hills of Vermont
and western Massachusetts, marveling at the beauty
of that place, and we went cross-country skiing
almost every day in the hills around our town,

and your mom wrote reviews of local art shows
and she put on exhibitions at our gallery and we made
good friends as I looked for jobs other places,
teaching jobs or anything that would take us away
from the darkness of loss that was defining us, no matter
what we did or how we laughed sometimes, a loss
that lived in the trees and snowfall and windowpanes,
in the buildings of that town, in the beautiful rivers
and waterfalls there. There was nothing we could do

but move, and so we gave up everything
and started the life we've been living thirty years

in tropical flatlands, salt marsh and everglade,
and we've made a family without you, dear daughter,

who've always been with us, I promise you, somewhere

deep in the blood, in the marrow, in the breath
we share each night, your mother and I,

in sleep, no matter what we're dreaming.

2.

And I think of a beautiful woman who lives
in the woods, a silent woman who lives

in the way the leaf of a birch tree might flutter
in the wind no one feels, or the way any stream

is full of dancers, full of living creatures
no one even sees except her, sweet woman

who moves by breathing, and never blows away,
though she seems like the wind, this woman who can't

be seen, although she is the gleaming
we love so, in water or mica, or in

the pale underbellies of fluttering leaves—

*

and when the first snow falls, she is that silence
that will melt into the ground before anything lands

or walks there, that silence that seeps down into
the earth and makes those bone-chilling rivers

we drink from sometimes when we're so thirsty

our words have dried up inside us, the words
that might save something real and true

if we could only speak them, and so we lean down

and drink from that freezing river, and dunk
our heads down under, and pull them out again

to sing to the world and each other, and then

3.

sitting in this garden, in this other country
we moved to so many years ago,

I look up at the evening settling around us,
damp and still, though the sky is still light.

Crows and ibis are flying east, just above our live oak trees,

toward their rookery islands in the bay.
Colleen's in the kitchen moving pots and pans around

as she thinks about dinner; the radio is chattering
contentedly. Soon I'll get up

and go inside to help her, but for now I'll just sit here
quietly, watching the birds, listening

carefully for the *woosh* of their beating wings,
softer than my own breath, as they fly toward the islands

just offshore
where they'll sing until it's dark.

Lesson

We all know stories of people who've turned into things
like trees, who woke up as an insect or a bear,
a river or a whole field of flowers.
And of course we've heard stories of people turned to ashes
and snow—snow falling, snow covering the ground
in deep drifts we could tunnel through, almost disappearing there.

One winter the snow was so deep in our town
we had to climb out our windows and up
to the surface, a vast expanse with just
the top branches of a few tall trees sticking through.

If we fell through the crust, we might tumble through the white
too deep to climb back out. There were birds in mid-flight there
and dogs standing still, as though the snow had caught them
in a flash. But when the snow melted, years later,

everything returned to normal, though the rivers
were swollen at first with dogs and debris.
There were ponds in the woods for a few weeks; they became
fields of flowers when they vanished, full of buzzing bees
which taught us something else, something harder.

Elegy

We walked through the dark city, talking
about the things that mattered to us then:
the most vivid ways to live, how to keep the fire
ablaze inside; the girls we'd loved, the women
we'd meet someday. We might even build
a house, we dreamed, with all our other friends,
out in the country, or maybe we'd move
to some other country, away from all the clutter
and flash. We smoked a joint and sat
on a stoop and sang to the darkness. We'd decided
to walk till first light, for the mild adventure
of watching an entire winter night.

Toward dawn we passed a church looming
in the darkness and stopped to admire it, and heard
someone singing inside, high pitched
and thin as the glow from the moon against
those stained-glass windows. We stood still
to listen as snow flurries started.
We watched our breath rise and mingle in the yellow
light, the buzzing of the streetlamps
as loud as her voice. I wanted to sing back to her,
but she would never hear, so I started
to hum. You hugged me then on the sidewalk,

old friend, in your peacoat; you kissed my frozen ears,
my forehead. Your breath smelled like wet wool—I remember
that well, after all these years—and you told me
you loved me. I said the same to you,
though I couldn't have meant it. Did you? We were just boys.

The Drink

In some other world, lost now, my grandfather
stands in his vegetable garden in shorts
with knee socks and bow tie, a pipe clamped between
his teeth and a straw hat on his head, and tells me

stories about animals, one turtle in particular
who visits every summer. My grandfather talks
in a monotone when he has that pipe clamped so tightly,
so I don't understand exactly what he's saying

though I know he's telling stories to delight me, and stories
about snakes too, their shed skins. He is always formal
in his manners, though his stories are wild.
Now I tell him I love to shoot arrows in the fields,

up into the sky. He nods once and smiles.
When I tell him I found some mushrooms in the woods
he says I'll have to show him, and when I tell him

there are boulders in the woods, with puddles that stay there
for many days after it rains, he tells me
if I drink from a puddle like that I can grow
frogs in my belly that will stay there all my life,

and he asks me to take him there, so we can share a drink.

The Prayer

My father whispered to himself in the morning
as he walked around the warm house balancing his coffee,
before the rest of the family had awakened.
There were geese and seagulls outside, in the snow,
and he watched them for a while from the living room window
while the train in the distance moved off, toward the city,
full of men like him, reading newspapers. Sometimes
I woke too and stood unseen behind him.
The house was still sleeping. I was trying to hear
what he said in the half-dark, before he went upstairs,
still talking to himself like a prayer, to get dressed for work.
There are bare trees in the words I am speaking here now,
that stood in the backyard, trees full of winter birds
he would scatter stale bread crumbs for as they gathered
at the suet he had hung for them there.
And I could have climbed those trees in that backyard
in spring and sat very quietly, and almost
disappeared, at least for a while, but by then
I was full of silence, like my father must have been,
and needed to whisper all the time.

The Open House

Then one afternoon, we opened all the windows
of that big suburban house to the autumn's chill
and let it blow through, while we walked from room
to room just feeling that weather.

Outside the cool in the trees was delicious
and their branches held migrating birds that sang
as they rested, but we were entranced by the cool
that scoured our living room. And then my father played

a Benny Goodman tune he'd loved in the navy,
"Sing! Sing! Sing!"—the one with the Gene Krupa
solo to start it, a song that's almost
forgotten by now. Standing there in the darkening

living room as the breezes whipped through, I could see
his eyes glistened brightly as he listened, though
I knew he wasn't crying—he'd loved that tune
in the navy he told us again, when he was

just a kid from Brooklyn. "Look at me now,"
he said with a smile in his voice, and I think
he danced a little, though I couldn't tell for sure
since the room was truly dark by then. And then he put it on again.

Before the Day Grows Warm

Now a covey of birds whose name I don't know
chatters down from the gumbo-limbo tree
I sit beneath, reading Chinese poetry.

Everyone else in my family is still sleeping.
The gardenia has blossomed for the first time in years
and the blossoming jasmine swarms with bees
whose buzzing I can hear
from clear across the garden.

The highest good is like clear water . . .

Sometimes, as it grows older,
my body reminds me of a stranger I've met
on some back road at dusk, who asks if he can walk
beside me, smiles through broken teeth,
and starts to tell his story.

Before long I've left him behind, though I still hear
his voice in the distance, if I listen. *Not now.*

Instead I get up and go back into the house
to wake my family, which causes the birds
to burst into the sky, which causes the tree
to quiver and sing, then fall silent.

Systems of Vanishing (excerpt)

Our days can line up one after another
or they can be shuffled like a deck of cards.

We can look through our days
like we'd look through a window,
a set of binoculars, or list of "things to do."

Our days can roll forward like breakers in a storm
or lap toward high tide
on a calm summer morning.

The days of our lives can be a long saunter
through scenery we know well, with companions we love,

or they can be more like a short walk alone,
lost but amazed at the scenery.

Selections from
The Frozen Harbor

The Ghosts

I love to sit up late, reading any book
whose words are erased by my reading, until
I imagine I'm actually wind who's learned
to stop, or rain that denies its own wetness
until it can gather itself into an animal
no one's ever seen, a hairy fist
of a creature, like someone concocted from the dust
on the wings of a moth, a dust-man covered
in miniscule bits of mica that gleam
like silent explosions. In other words, I love
long lost poems by anonymous ghosts
who lived so ascetically they practiced breathing
like trees, and lay down in mountain creeks
to emerge with ice for eyes: *My transparent*
wings flutter when you stroke them someone
whispers as he asks us to think about the darkness
we enter when we blink, and he asks us to blink
more slowly, so we can spend more time
in mushroom-growing light, that twilight through which
another moon rises, pulling healing tides
through the bodies we've forgotten, and schools of just-spawned
minnows beyond our mind's terrain
shiver and dart in the darkness.

Extinction

The creature my mother had been once was hiding
in a supermarket magazine photograph, as though
she were a stylish shoe; the animal my father
had fancied as *himself*, was howling at the moon
like the wolf in that famous ad campaign
that taught us how to act wild and stylish at once,
like a new kind of gesture. We had lost all the creatures
that weren't of our ilk, like we'd lost certain aunts
and uncles to their snapshots. And then we started losing
those animals inside us, as our sleep started dreaming
in languages of follicle and cuticle, fingernail
and earwax, sand and snot. Until something
moved around inside again, wilder than we'd ever been
and almost as vivid as the world, and it hurt
like language must have done once, or maybe even love.

Baby Mammals

1.

Many evenings for the past few months, an opossum
has climbed up into our back-door garbage can
to sleep. I've watched from the sunroom window
as he's shuffled across our back porch
to leap up and climb in, careful not to tip it over.

On more than one still-dark morning I've startled him
into a posture of death—eyes glazed,
tail stiff, legs akimbo—as I've thrown something in there,
on him, without thinking. He's almost petite—
he'd easily fit into a shoebox—so I think of him

as an adolescent. And I feel oddly proud
that he's chosen our house for a home. What dreams
shiver his body, nestled there in our garbage,
while we putter through the house, or dream our own worlds
just a few feet away?

2.

The first time I woke to my parents fighting
the way they did sometimes when they drank, in voices
I didn't recognize, slurred and dripping spite,
I slipped out of bed, stood at the head
of the stairs and listened, terrified, not
knowing who they were now. Then I slipped back into
a private kind of silence, waiting for my dreams.

I listened to those strange voices even as I slept,
for years, in that comfy bed alone.

Sometimes I woke up before morning—just in case—
and listened to the quiet house beathing, and listened
to the night creatures moving outside through the dark,
sniffing and scratching for food.

The Field

I woke that dawn to ghost horses standing
in the trees at the edge of our field,
watching our house from the sides of their faces
and fading as I walked out through the cold wet grass
to welcome them. Still, there were hoof prints in the dirt
by the trees, and still there was a sweet smell
hanging in the first light, and a stillness.

I don't know how to behave around horses.

But you, my love, have ridden from the darkness
of dawn to the darkness of evening on a horse,
on a thin road whose name you have tried to forget.
So I didn't tell you about them.

Instead I let you sleep until the day had settled
into its small bodies. Your dreams had been a tunnel,
you told me, a dark seam through a mountain
where the wild creatures lived unaware of us humans
or as though they were the only real humans in the world.

That evening, I cut up apples and left them
by those trees, and soon the horses came.
There were hundreds of birds there too, telling stories
we couldn't understand yet, as we got up together

an walked through the tall grass in silence, scaring them
suddenly into the darkness.

Skin

When we opened our family photo albums
after our parents had died, we were
confused: we didn't recognize
anyone, not even ourselves.
The houses and vacation spots looked exactly
as we remembered, as did the pets, the cars
and the clothes the people in the pictures wore,
but the people themselves were strangers.

At the end of her life, my mother's skin
was so thin she bruised when she spoke and even
when she was kissed, so we kissed the air
and blew it toward her the way they do
in old movies just as they're leaving.

I can't remember who you are, Michael,
she told me, *though I know you are my son.*
We held hands and looked at each other. Her hand
quivered its bones like a starving broken bird.
When I told her I loved her, I couldn't meet her eyes.

Ceremony

Just as some underground aquifers hold
water that's older than language, which
we pump to green our lawns,

the dust that settles all around us is flecks
of skin and dander
that's blown around
and around the planet, to finally drift down
upon us. And just as we don't notice it
falling, we wipe it away

without thinking, though lately I do imagine
my brother must circle the planet now
as dust from the smoke
that rose from his body.

I think of him drifting high and far away
and I think of the rain somewhere that will carry
those tiny flakes of flesh down
to grass and earth. Or maybe he'll simply
drift down through the air to land on a table
or chair so someone can dust him away.

Sometimes I see him huddling inside
a snowflake that floats in the air of a not-quite
winter afternoon of flurries, to melt
on still-unfrozen ground.
I love the way those first flakes dance so gently down.

The Frozen Harbor

One blue-tinted winter afternoon, when the harbor
we lived beside seemed to have frozen solid,
my brother and I ventured out onto that salt-ice,
which groaned and shifted as the tide rose
or fell below us and our mother called
from shore *please come in*. Of course we pretended
we were too far out to hear her. As evening
settled around us, we started talking
in a language we made up as we spoke, a language
we grew more fluent in as we kept talking.
We lay down together on our backs on the ice,
in silence, and looked up into the sky,
and listened as a stillness settled into the hollows
inside us—I still feel it sometimes, even
after all these years. Then we stood up
and reluctantly leaned toward shore, talking
softly now, pulling the star-filled
darkness behind us, willing our bodies
to be lighter than they really were, feeling the light
inside us and the dark water pulling just below.

Saturday Morning

All those caterpillars ravaging the milkweed
in the pot on your back porch—you can hear them chewing
even as you play your guitar to the squirrels
and doves, to the invisible stars and the oak trees
that cast their pollen across the scraggle-grass
that yearns to grow thorns and wildflowers, as you
sing out of tune to the bananas just starting
to push their fingers into the gloves
of their skin. Inside the house, your clothes
are sleeping in their closets, your shoes are dozing
to the scent of your feet in their cracks and pores
while the ceiling fan flutters some wisps of hair
that fall across the face of the sleeping woman
who happens to be dreaming of crows higher up
in those backyard trees, watching you play
and laughing into their feathers as a cat
slinks from the bushes to pounce on a dove
feasting from the feeder the squirrels have knocked
to the ground, then carrying the fluttering bird
to its own yard, next door, to show the children
who live there its proud accomplishment.
But you've seen the whole thing, so you chase the damn cat,
guitar cradled gently, and it drops the wounded bird
to the grass where it flutters, broken but not dead yet,
and you wonder for a moment if you can turn away,
then decide you'll have to kill it, and wonder
how to do that, with a shovel or big rock,
as the woman who was sleeping steps out the back door,
groggy and still in her nightgown, to tell you
her dream and to thank you whose singing made her
feel purely happy for a moment as she woke
and just lay there in her body beside where you'd lain
in that bed, as you do every night, and she just wants
to thank you; she holds out her arms for a hug
as you cast your eyes around for a safe place to put
your guitar down so you can return her affection
before that sweet moment has passed.

The Happiness of Trees

I slept that summer on a screen porch in the woods
    with the creatures and insects singing so loudly
my mind seemed to join them—out there without me—
    to move around like the breeze from form to form

and then to return as a fox or a cicada,
    some other night creature, to slip back inside me
humming whatever it had heard, patterns
    I couldn't sing along with but felt inside

like the happiness of trees when a soft wind
    turns their leaves' pale underbellies to the sky
and makes the sap rise. I love to wake
    before myself, to silence and fog.

Sometimes I got up and walked out into the chilly woods
    and sometimes I turned over as though this happiness
might last forever, and slept just a while
    longer, until the first birds sang.

Selections from
Sleeping with the Lights On
Bluer and More Vast

That Stranger's Continent

I wonder how many microscopic creatures live inside my body, eating other tiny creatures in there, creating other little creatures, making waste and growing hungry. I've heard that there are whole nations of such creatures in every organ and orifice, and I've heard that these creatures are specific to me, or to you—that is, since they've evolved with us they can live only in us; they think and dream and move and sing specifically as creatures within us. I'd bet there are more creatures inside each of us than there are people in the world. Imagine finding yourself somehow amongst that crowd, inside your own body, shrunk to their size. Would you feel hopelessly lost, or might you recognize someone from your past? Might you call out to him in your new language? And might he turn to you then with a squint and a shrug and suddenly break out smiling?

When I lived in the city, I'd occasionally bump into someone I'd almost totally forgotten. Wending through the midtown crowds during rush hour, some man or woman about my age would knock into me as though purposefully, step back and yelp a name. Sometimes that name was mine, in which case I'd suddenly remember him or her and we'd stand there talking while the crowds rushed past. We'd exchange our phone numbers then, kiss or shake hands fondly and step back into the fray.

One evening, I bumped into a woman I'd played hide-and-seek with, once, maybe twice, when our parents had a barbeque. I'd hid in the bushes with her. She'd held my hand. I don't remember if we were ever caught or if we made it home free. I do know that as I spoke to her, twenty-five years later, I remembered her smell, like suntan lotion, that had lingered on my own hand after hers had pulled away. Here she was standing in the street in the city-dusk, talking about her husband and children, her full and perfectly ordinary life. When we kissed chastely in parting, we must have shared at least a few microscopic creatures that had been only ours, until we kissed. Maybe some small number of our tiniest selves survived, in that foreign country, that stranger's continent, and are hiding in the darkness of that hide-and-seek still, breathing each other's sweet blossoming, hoping no one will find them.

To Sing the World

Whenever I travel, the birds tell me first I'm in new country.
—Gary Young

1.

Some mornings when I step outside to fetch the paper, the
darkness feels laden with the damp scents of the night as the
night itself seeps into the ground. Every once in a while I startle
an opossum and sometimes a whole possum family as they sniff
through the bushes, heading home—wherever home is—to sleep.
I imagine them sleeping as a single ball of gray fur, and I wonder
what they smell like, sleeping there, underneath my house maybe,
or behind some familiar bushes. I wonder how their breath
sounds as they sleep. Often lately I wake in the middle of the
night, startled by my own breathing, or by a dream. I lie there
and listen to the hum my wife's sleeping body makes, and I listen
to the clicks and shifts inside the darkness. Sometimes I grow
frightened, lying there, and sometimes I realize I have wasted my
life. Not all of it, of course, but a substantial sum. Certain birds
fly only at night, small migrating songbirds that feel safe in the
darkness. They land at first dawn in the quivering trees and sing
out their adventures to each other and the world.

2.

Someone is singing from inside a house along our street, but
I can't determine which house her voice is coming from. She
sings beautifully, but more than *beauty,* her voice conveys an
urgency not of pain or pleasure but of something more deeply
haunting, as though someone could sing inside a tree or a stone.
Or inside a bird, for that matter, inside a bird's bones, inside
a bird's bones as that bird flies south, inside a bird's bones as
that bird lands and sings. I walk up and down the street leaning
toward each house, stilling my breath, listening, as the evening
settles around us. As usual, there's no one else in the street; as
usual, the houses are closed up around their secrets, as though
the lives inside them were fleshless but yearning, like pollen on
the breeze of a summer's afternoon.

3.

Our own house is surrounded by trees and bushes, each of which is filled with small vivid lives that are aware of us as we might be aware of many futures, potential but unformed. They don't know what we are, but they hear us moving back and forth, yelling out and lumbering across the grass. They flicker into hiding when we come too close. Eventually they may learn to ignore us. Everything we do must seem oblivious to them, the lizards and ants, spiders and snakes, all of whom have to live by their wits and are granted no second chances. Those small birds too, those butterflies and bees. When we watch them I think they must feel an unnerving pull, as though they were drowning but still able to breathe, as though a strange energy were rearranging everything just a little, including the air.

4.

Once as a child I walked through a field of tall grass to a row of dark trees whose air was so cool it frightened me a little. The mushrooms looked like the bones of someone who wasn't completely decomposed, and the house I'd walked from looked hazy in the distance, as if it were floating slightly off the ground. So I picked up a twig and kissed it to give it magic, then hid it beneath a loaf-sized stone and started back to the house. As I walked back, I saw my father and grandfather, smoking pipes, walking toward me through the grass. They were talking, both of them, with their teeth firmly clamped on their pipes, so their voices sounded muffled and annoyed. But they weren't annoyed at all! They'd found a turtle in the front garden and they wanted to show me. So I held their hands and we walked back together through that tall grass that was buzzing now with dragonflies and hummingbirds. I loved the smell of their pipe smoke. My grandfather smelled of hair oil and leather, which I loved too. My brother was napping in that big house, alone in the bed we shared, surrounded by feathers we'd collected every morning before the dew had dried. My mother was reading on the shady back porch, reading and crying until she'd disappeared, while her mother—my grandma—snapped bones for the broth we would sip so discreetly after cocktails in the den. There were crows in the attic, like old photograph albums, singing their darkness, an ancient tapestry. Since the windows were open, they could fly out when they needed to, pulling the night-world behind them.

5.

I've heard this: In every cell there's something like a universe, energies and relationships that function like our stars and planets, like our light and lives. And these cells, in relationship, are the only world we can truly know. But what about the universe inside each of these cells? Could we somehow, someday, slip in there and live, for one tiny moment, as a moment in that universe? What would we see there? And what about those cells inside the cells inside us? Are they virtual universes too? What's time there? What's distance? What's love? Inside our bodies, in the secret places, there are large-shouldered animals moving slowly through the tall grass, watched over by wolves whose breath can be seen as the dusk-air grows cool. There has never been a human there, but somehow we can listen to the shuffle of these huge beasts' legs as they move, we can hear their hooves step lightly. That's how many of them there are right now inside us, moving across the landscape. Each heartbeat in each of their bodies beats inside us, deeper than anyone has ever ventured, or ever will.

6.

I'm out of fire, someone says to the trees, *and I'm almost out of air*. I see him standing there on the sidewalk; hear him from my lawn chair nestled almost in the bushes. Now he leans and picks up a pebble, marble-shoots it straight up in the air and stands

there watching it rise and fall, a man about my age, who hasn't
noticed me. Then he mutters, *oh the hell with it,* and walks
quickly on, as though going somewhere in a hurry. I am reading
Jack Gilbert, who died a few months ago, listening carefully to
his language-carvings in the still air, wondering at the urgency
of everything he said, at the seed-urgent pull of his need for
primal love, the love that makes us cry in our fingerprints and
teeth, for the taste of the mica in the stone. I know so few of the
creatures all around me, buzzing and humming and yearning
to eat me, going about their supremely healthy lives. I am only
what I am now, fragments of the larger breath. And no one else
passes on the sidewalk for hours, and no one else drives down
the street, though many birds continue to fly overhead, some so
high all I can see of them is blue.

7.

And if I took the same walk every day for a year, what would
I see there and who would I be? There is evidence of broken
bones, broken bottles, broken wings. Everywhere we look there
are reasons to go home. If I took the same walk every day for a
decade, one phase of my life to another, would I learn something
valuable about memory and pain? I am almost myself almost all
of the time, almost never completely. But what does that mean to
the mouse in my study, behind the chair I read in, and what does
that matter to the wind through the trees, which ruffles the fur
on the squirrel who chatters at the shadows moving across the
lawn? The grass in another world grows without stopping, grows
deeper and deeper until each blade is like a tree, and the forest
is tight and flimsy and green, and the light that shines through it
feels hollow, like a bone. Mind is a dream, like the moon in the
trees when the trees shift and sway, just a little, in the breeze. Is
there anything anywhere that lives without mind? Is that snail
not singing as he glides across the sidewalk into the fresh-cut,
dewy evening grass?

The Ordinary Wonders

Taking out the compost after days of rain, I almost walk
through the freshly-woven spiderweb stretched between two
palm trees. So I slowly lean the compost down and kneel there
watching, to see what that spider's up to. There's a female
cardinal in the still-dripping firecracker bush that stretches out
above my head, and I wonder if she might be the same little
bird who flapped against my study window a few hours ago,
then tumble-wrestled with another bird before flying off. I'm
watching the spiderweb but nothing's happening, so I blow
softly across it, meaning no harm, and out scampers the spider
from behind a shriveled leaf, into the center of his web. Is he
looking up at me? I stop blowing. Clouds are moving quickly
across the sky. I can feel them as I stand here watching my
spider, who watches his human. And now a real breeze awakens
in the trees, quivering the web. Unlike my breath, the breeze
doesn't seem to alarm the little spider in the least. He walks
now, *strolls* we might even say, back to his shriveled leaf and
slips under. And as I lean down to pick up the bowl of scraps
I hear my neighbor singing next door, a full-throated jingle of
lust and abandon. So I hold myself still, just to listen.

The Flood

*You're capturing something elusive, something
you're not always sure of, and you're trying to
capture it before it vanishes.*
　　　　—Philip Pearlstein

1.

During a lull in the rain, I took a walk to the marsh, just to be
outside, and found a bedraggled little dog running circles around a
man who lay amidst a clutter of tide debris. He wore an overcoat,
shoes without socks, and refused help or money before I'd offered.
When he asked my name I remembered my parents and answered
don't have one, then asked about the dog: why was he so small;
why didn't he bark? But the man said the runt wasn't his, was just
another kind of lie I hadn't learned to tell yet. He told me he didn't
have a name either, that he stayed too busy to indulge in such
vanity. Then he turned away, sighing, and fell back to sleep, and
the rain resumed falling, even harder than before.

So I ran home, followed by that secret little dog.

By the time I arrived, the water had risen into the kitchen;
my parents were lolling on the floor, splashing each other and
trying to teach my little sister how to swim. In the living room
my brother sat naked in water up to his chin and watched our
brand-new color TV, which seemed to work fine, even half-
submerged: Another sort of miracle. The house smelled of turkey
and mashed potatoes, fresh-brewed coffee and apple pie.

Then my parents were doing the dead man's float, holding
their breath so long that my sister was quietly starting to cry.
In another room the phone was ringing, so I waded down the
hallway to answer, hoping it would fall silent before I arrived.

2.

So much rain this year, she tells us, fish have started surfacing
from their deep pools underground, up through caves and coral
and soil, into the puddles that are flooding our gardens. When

I wade through the back yard to the alley to dump the garbage,
fish thrash and splash me and sometimes cause me to drop
the garbage bag, which they ravenously rip to shreds. Soon
we may be swimming off our back porch. Then the rains will
stop, as they always do in winter, and we will plant our garden,
fertilized this year by the fish which will have died and rotted—
unless they are able to slip back down into their underground
grottoes. Pelicans and anhinga have landed in our oak trees.

3.

Do you feel the deep breaths that move through your body, she
wonders, do you know who sings at the back of your head? My
memory is faulty, but my hopes are eternal, like the foxes that set
out at dusk. They dance and forage around our neighborhood
while we're shut up inside eating dinner. And when I say *dance*, I
mean it, she says: have you ever seen them jump for a bird which
has swooped low to the ground, and catch it?

She tells us she understands music much more deeply since that
afternoon she fell off the high dive while no one was looking,
hit her head on a kick board in the water and went down.
Now she knows harmony and dissonance as well as she knows
how to chew her food; she knows all the words of all the jazz
standards and even the most obscure operas, in their original
languages. She says she doesn't even *like* that kind of music and
starts to sing in other voices, back and forth, in harmony.

4.

We sat at the end of a concrete pier that stretched out into the
St. Johns River and watched black skimmers circle, bottom half
of their beaks zipping through the water, making a soft *hiss*, like
gentle rain. In the grasses behind us, tall white birds stood still.

Years later we paddled kayaks out to a sand bar slung between two small islands where we could wade, watch birds, and gather shells. The water slapped from both directions, sending claps of small waves up into mist and breeze. We sat in the water there, rocking back and forth. Plovers flew near, rose up and fell into the waves, catching tiny food. A bedraggled pelican flew by, stabbing the swells but catching only water. High above, vultures and magnificent frigate birds moved in slow circles, almost out of sight.

5.

So I lie back in the water and look up at the sky and wonder what I would say to you if we met today as strangers living one of the many different lives we could so easily have entered, many times, with one of our other loves. I think you'd live in Colorado or California, and I might have ended up anywhere. We'd both be married, and I think we'd both have children—so our own children wouldn't exist, except as other people. Maybe we'd both be spending a few nights here on the beach on our way somewhere else. There'd be a summer storm and our sons, who would be about the same age, would rent boards and surf the larger-than-usual waves while we stood at shore's edge and watched. You'd have a pair of binoculars I'd borrow to watch them. I think I'd notice your eyes. Maybe your husband would be sleeping off a bad mood and maybe my beautiful wife would be having her fingernails painted again. Maybe I'd ask you to body surf with me, which you would demurely decline, since you wouldn't swim well; and maybe it would start raining hard enough to make the sand dance and our sons hoot in joy.

I see them out there now, floating out beyond the swells on their rented surfboards, laughing and yelling back and forth to each other with the same vivid energy that connected us, so many years ago. They don't even know each other's names.

Or maybe your son meets my daughter somewhere else, in another city where she's living for the summer while she studies anthropology, art history, simple food and love. Maybe he asks her to take a walk with him. It's beautiful there, walking at dusk beside that river, watching swallows scribble and dance.

Maybe they talk about their parents as they walk, or maybe they don't say anything at all.

for Colleen Ahern-Hettich, and for Tom Virgin

The Hurricane

Last night while we slept, someone stole all our windows. They unscrewed the frames and pulled the glass from the wall, made our house into a cave with many awkward entrances. I woke this morning to the cooing of mourning doves in our bedroom, the patter of rain on the floors. I got up and wandered the house in a daze, examining our garden through the empty window frames. I leaned my head out into that emptiness and let the rain drench me.

Then I threw a book out there, through the empty picture window, into the sodden grass. It was a book I'd disliked for a long time, a classic, and it felt good to see it splayed out there in the rain. I searched through my bookshelves for other books I detested. Then I went around, still undressed, pitching other objects out through this window or that: knickknacks and junk mail, cheap vases, old shoes. I stood as far back from each window as possible and threw hard, like the pitcher I'd once imagined I could be.

When my clamor woke the children, they helped me scatter bird seed on the furniture and carpets. We made bird baths from the cups and cereal bowls, grottoes for nests where the books had lived, lined up alphabetically for easy reference—as though the life I'd imagined I had built could be organized by author and made to cohere. We decided to wait a while before we woke their mom.

A breeze was moving briskly through the house by then, and all sorts of brightly-colored birds were arriving. My wife wasn't up yet but I knew she'd be pleased to see them gathered there, singing, making nests. I knew she'd be happy we'd scattered that seed, pleased with the way we'd transformed our house from disaster to refuge while she'd been sleeping. The breeze smelled like night-blooming jasmine and orange blossoms, fragrances that make us feel happy and alive. I sat watching birds roost in my living room, listening to my children as they walked through the garden, cooing and gathering the junk I'd thrown out there, crying out now and then at their useless broken toys.

The Houses

So many families have started living in our trees: when we walk through our neighborhood in the evenings, we hear whispering above our heads, and the rustling of bodies that aren't owls or squirrels. The houses that were once so well maintained are empty now, their lawns unkempt, their mailboxes overflowing with fliers and magazines, their windows broken. Who knew such solid dreams could fall so quickly to ruin? The packs of stray dogs are mostly harmless, though they make messes no one cleans up, so we shoo them from our yard, whose two huge oaks hold families we've gotten to know, at least a little, since the adjustment began. We sometimes bring them food, and they watch things for us, when we have to go out for some reason.

It's strange to still be living in a house, after almost everyone else has moved into the trees, but it holds all our books and musical instruments, and where would we—*who* would we—be without those precious things? I know I'm no musician, but still I love to play. I sit at night, even now, strumming my guitar, while my family and the tree-families sing along with me.

Since the humans have taken over the trees and the meadows and the woods, the birds we love have had nowhere to live, so we've transformed our rooms into wild places for them, we've opened our windows to let them fly in, fly home as it were, since we've made these places real—or real enough, it seems, to convince these lovely creatures. Often now, in the afternoon, I sit playing my guitar while the people outside in the sunny summer trees debate questions like which of the candidates might restore their savings and their televisions, which candidate might figure out how to keep the wind out of their branches.

Inside our bird-filled house, the woods and fields stretch farther each day, in response to those birds and our singing. There will be migrations this year, for the first time, inside a house. And soon enough the forest will stretch so many miles, our children will be able to venture out with only their gumption and start a new life there, for themselves and their families, all in this house we've refused to leave. And maybe, if what we are doing here is noticed, other families will move back into their old homes, restore the rooms and animals like we have, until slowly each house will become itself again, alive and aching with its ancient mysteries of fur, and pollen, and dust.

The Other Woman

Walking home through the early dark, carrying yellow flowers for his wife, he passed a car parked half on the sidewalk and half in the street. As he walked around it he could see that it was filled with moths, which beat gently against the windows, as though they could slip through and fly up to the streetlight. The street was quiet. He cupped his free hand against the driver's side window and looked in: the car was otherwise empty. He looked around: all the buildings lining the street were dark, and though the sky was still light, it would soon be fully dark as well. He tried the car's door and was surprised to find it open. Surely those moths would want to fly free. What should he do? He thought of his wife and the flowers he'd bought her, that would make her so happy, at least for a moment. He set them down on the pavement and slipped into the car, waving his hands to shoo the moths free. He would do this for a few minutes, then get out and walk home with his flowers. Maybe she was cooking something special for him, right now, or maybe she'd opened a fresh bottle of wine. She'd love the fact that he'd thought of her, that he'd gotten just the kind of flowers she loved most. But instead of flying free, the moths had started landing on his face, in his hair. They stuck themselves to him so tightly he couldn't wave them loose; when he brushed at them more violently their guts smeared all over his hair and shirt. What a mistake! Just a minute ago he'd been smartly groomed; now he was covered in moth-gunk and wing-dust. So he stepped out of the car and picked up his flowers, which were only slightly worse for the wear. He slammed the car door and turned to walk home with some of those moths still clinging to him, as the car's alarm let forth a huge siren, which echoed up and down the street, causing other car alarms to wail loudly in response. And the moths beat against him as though he were a street light even as he started running, chased now by a beautiful woman he hadn't noticed before, who swung a butterfly net around her head and cried "Stop! It's hopeless! You'll never get away!"

The Purposeful Hum

At first I couldn't believe the news that scientists had discovered a way to ascertain *why* each of us was born, by pricking us slightly through the moons of our thumbs and putting that tiny specimen under a high-powered microphone that can actually detect sound that lies deeper than genetics—these scientists call it *purposeful humming*. Then they amplify this sound by a billion until they can hear its harmonics. It's somewhere in these haunting harmonies that they've been able to isolate the code, the secret, to our purpose, the role we were born to fulfill. Soon, one of these scientists says, we'll be able to prick our newborns so they won't waste time trying to "find themselves," and eventually we might even be able to prick babies in utero and design our cities, our very society, by responding to what we hear there.

There's a pattern to everything, of course, including time, so it follows that birds and butterflies might be trained to fly through time without necessarily flying through space. You see? The possibilities are as exciting as discovering another organ inside the body, a sponge-like part of ourselves that can soak up the memories we don't want anymore and squeeze them back out as newly-minted fractals of experience that make us feel so good we might almost say we're happy.

It's like the time our subway stopped beneath the river. The doors slid open and everyone got out, pulled back the curtains of darkness that hung there and walked into a place and time where they were exactly who they should have been, even if they should have been ugly or alone, which hardly ever happened, or they should have been a dog, or a bat, or a field mouse, which did in fact happen, more often than you might expect.

And then the curtain closed again, and the empty train moved forward through the dark.

Until It Grows Too Dark

My silence is walking through a strange city in the rain, a city whose language he doesn't understand. He has no money in his pockets. His wallet holds only snapshots. My silence is walking because there's nothing else to do; he's not looking for anything particular; he's not sure where he is. His own silence, which is buried far deeper inside him, tells him to keep walking, keep looking. *Something will show itself*, his silence seems to say. This man, my silence, loves to read stories to his children, sitting in the garden in the late afternoon. Now, in this strange city, he steps into a bodega to ask for help but feels suddenly too shy to approach the stern-looking woman at the cash register or the skinny kid mopping the floor. So my silence steps back out into the rain. He keeps walking while his own silence reassures him everything will be alright. Eventually he finds a small park with benches sheltered beneath a lean-to where he can sit out of the rain. Except for a few pigeons, the park is empty. And as he sits there, he grows indistinct, until he looks more like a smudge than a man.

Back where he comes from his wife and children have gathered as usual in the garden. His wife holds the book he read from yesterday. His son is impatient: he yearns to tell his dad about this girl, his classmate, who put her head down on her desk and fell so deeply asleep no one could wake her. He wants to explain how she'd spoken in her sleep, how she'd said something to him. He whispers her name. Soon the crickets and night creatures are calling back and forth and the small family is invisible in the darkness. The mother's voice is still whispering a story, but soon she too will fall silent.

Waking to Rain

*I thought about the secrets our bodies have, what they
keep from us. Our bodies have lives of their own.*
        —John Dufresne

When I was a child, my hands would sometimes fall off and get lost
in the grass or in my house somewhere—and I would have to search
for them, sometimes late at night, when everyone else was sleeping.
I'd be lying in bed, starting to drift off, when I'd need to touch my
own body, and I'd realize my hands were missing. So I'd lie there
trying to remember back to when I'd used them last. After a while
I'd get up, get dressed as best I could without hands, and I'd walk
around the dark house, out into the yard and street, looking for my
hands, calling out—until at last I found them. Once I lost my hands
for a whole winter afternoon when I hadn't worn gloves. They had
to be thawed out slowly, under lukewarm water. They ached for
days. Another time I lost them in a puddle in a thunderstorm, and
by the time I found them they were milk-colored, swollen, clumsy,
and heavy—like waterlogged wood. Once I lost a hand when I
was body surfing; and once my right hand snapped off in the grip
of one of my father's business associates, a man who believed in
shaking with authority. No one noticed, of course, except me. And
I yearned to learn an instrument, to sing and play music—but I
couldn't train my hands, couldn't trust them to follow me. Most
sports were pure embarrassment. Of course I never flew a kite!
Picture me walking home from elementary school: I'd drop a hand
like a Kleenex, without noticing until I'd reached home and I wasn't
able to open the front door. By that time my lost hand had crawled
away somewhere difficult to find. So I kept my hands in my pockets
and I tried not to let go of anything. Later, when I started dating, I
dreamed I'd let my girlfriend keep my hands overnight as a token of
my love, and I imagined my hands lying on her bedside table, beside
the glass of water and the book of Rod McKuen poems I'd given
her. Sometimes I imagined she took my hands into the shower, into
the bubble bath with her. She talked to my hands as though they
were sweet dolls; she scrubbed my fingernails; she traced my life line.
Then she used my hands to wash everywhere I imagined while I hurt
myself with blunt wrists in the potent darkness.

Windows, Mirrors, Chandeliers

Yesterday, riding our bikes in the Everglades, my wife and I noticed a large group of vultures about 100 yards ahead, hopping around a carcass. A man with a camera stood amongst them, but they seemed to pay him no attention. As we approached the group we could see that the birds were tearing the last bits of flesh from the skeleton of a huge alligator, the bones of whose tail lay scattered across the narrow road. The photographer smiled quietly as we passed, so still that the vultures had forgotten he was there. They started landing again as soon as we'd passed. Of course I thought of Tibetan sky burials, the sacred vultures that so thoroughly clean the human carcasses set out for them that the bones are scoured, denuded of the ichors of flesh. How high do those sacred birds fly, shitting their human remains across the land?

Somewhere, I've heard, they've developed a way of cremating the body and mixing a small amount of the beloved's ash into panes of glass, so those who still live will be able to look *through* their beloved, through glass that is only slightly foggy with the eternally-preserved fragments of bone and sinew, those precious remains. Might a whole house be equipped with windows tinted with loved ones' ashes, stained glass windows of a sort, grayish or flecked with fur-like particles? The kitchen windows might be cloudy with father's dust, while ashy smudges of mother's dark hair might dye the bedroom dormers. We could look through our loved ones as we looked out at the world. So every house we lived in might feel like church again, and looking out through our windows might become a form of prayer.

Sunday Morning

We were reading a story about William Thompson, the English-born railway worker who feigned death while he was scalped by Cherokees, who lived to retrieve his scalp after it fell from a warrior's belt, put it in a pail of water and even tried to have doctors sew it back on his head. Before he died, many years later, he mailed that scalp to the Omaha library, and they put it on display. His hair is still healthy-looking and gleaming on its dried-up scalp. We were reading aloud about Witold Pilecki, the Polish hero who walked voluntarily into Auschwitz in 1940 and stayed for three years, documenting what he saw. We were reading that the oceans are rising more quickly than predicted. We were reading about the eyesight of swifts and kites, of hawks and eagles and crows. We were reading a review of that movie about the strange planet hurtling toward the earth, how the power would fail and cars wouldn't start and people would have trouble breathing. We were only half-reading about the music of Wagner's later period. Instead, we were reading about Susan Sontag's diaries, how grandiose and self-involved she was. We were skimming a review of a book about John Berryman, who was even more grandiose and self-involved; about sculptures in the snow that melt when the snow melts, whose melting is their truest form. Then we were reading about the vast rivers underground that gush out millions of gallons every hour. We were wistfully reading about a Japanese spa where we could drink small cups of green tea while we sat in a pool of warm water, being scrubbed or massaged, while the breeze fluttered the curtains which fell across the open door, to push them open wide enough for us to see the garden's rocks and sculpted waterfalls. We were reading small poems then, not quite haiku, of Basho and Dogen: *A snowy heron on the snowfield/where the winter grass is unseen/hides itself/in its own figure.* We were putting our reading aside and going out to putter in our garden, to listen to the cardinals and mockingbirds and mourning doves, to smell the spearmint we'd planted by the henna tree. It was raining then, softly, and we let ourselves get wet, soaked through to the skin, which belonged to us now.

Selections from
To Start an Orchard

Marimba

The man I wish I'd had the gumption to become
back when I was green and restless
requested that when he finally let go
his bones be fashioned into a kind of xylophone
and that the rest of him be buried
by the lake he loved.
He wished that his bones be played
on chilly autumn evenings when loons called
and leaves whispered a leathery language
as the wind prepared them to let go.
Beside the lake his sons could make a fire
and burn his clothes and books,
then roast whatever they could catch, and feast.
But he died before I noticed, fell away
as a propped-up scarecrow falls from his scaffold
or the way memories fall from our minds
and become like small animals, mice or voles,
that know there are hungry owls in the woods
but can't stand to stay in their cramped nests any longer
and need to take a look at the moon.

The Milky Way

If we could imagine that every word we speak
were an animal or insect, the last of a species
ever to be born, that the very act of speaking
brought extinction even before our words
had been heard and replied to, we might get a feeling
for the vanishings we witness but don't see. And if every
conversation were understood as a kind
of holocaust denuding whole landscapes, some people
would simply fall silent—as far as they could—
while most others would keep chattering on. Just imagine
the vast forests of lives, the near-infinity of forms
brought to a halt with a simple conversation.

I would be one of the talkers, despite
the fact that I knew what my talking destroyed.
And so I would mourn every word I said,
even while I argued passionately for silence
and for learning to honor the sacred diversity
of life. Imagine watching the stars
go out on a dark night in the far north, a clear night,
one after the other until the sky went black.

Once, when I was taking out the garbage, just walking
dully across my back yard, a huge bird—
as big as a vulture but glittering and sleek—
rose from the grass and flew into my body,
knocked the breath out of me, then flew up and away
with a powerful pull of its wings. I could hardly

see it in the darkness. Then it was just gone.

The Ghost Trees

And now a certain kind of scientist says
the weather in various parts of the world
is growing exhausted and just wants to lie down
for a nap, or maybe for a longer dose
of oblivion, so its dreams can be
re-spawned, its creatures large and small
replenished to wildness, the air re-folded
into its invisible origami, even
human language shot-through again
with sap. In the clear-cut woods—
raw ground and stumps—invisible trees
are learning to move from one place to another,
blurring paths and meadows; the people
who live there call them *fathers who turned
away without waving goodbye, and learned
to dance slowly;* they contrast them with the boulders
and rocks, who truly know how to dance
in slow time, even as the humans and the creatures
in fur and the creatures in feathers leave
their bodies and all the bodies they passed through
to arrive at now through eternities—but still
we pretend they cast shadows across the ground,
and still we pretend they bear fruit.

The Shells

As the tide rises, tiny shells
tumble and wait, and tumble. There is nothing
alive inside most of them
but the kind of light
in a room whose curtains have been drawn for years,
a room whose window
faces a street
where people sit late into the evenings at cafés
and the palm fronds flutter. Someone sits quietly
in that room most afternoons, listening
to the chatter, trying to hear a voice
she might recognize. At dusk she gets dressed,
goes down to the café, and drinks a glass of wine.
No one ever talks to her. Of course the ocean never stops
pulling its shells from the deep; some of them
still have creatures alive inside them,
even as they're stranded by the falling tide
to dry up and die, or be eaten by the little birds
who run along the beach, willets or terns,
or picked up by someone who admires their beauty
then throws them back into the ocean.

To Start an Orchard

Whatever silences we'd always maintained
we continued to nurture, like the fruit from a landscape
that was foreign to us, even after all these years,
a fruit we weren't sure whether to peel,
cook, or eat raw, which we kept on our windowsill
until it had withered and was somehow
beautiful, like a curiosity we'd collected on the beach
that reminded us of journeys, fathomless depths,
and yet was just a piece of fruit, desiccated and black,
curled like the pit of a dream, or a nut.
And so, when you spoke, or tried to, a small plant
emerged from its folds and darkness, delicate
and proud and needing to be watered until
it could be planted outside. I could already
hear the birds singing from its wilderness of branches.
I was already humming to the buzzing of its bees.

The Light of Ancient Stars

The kid in the newspaper article had calculated
    the number of human beings who'd lived
since the moment the first one emerged from the not-quite-
    human woman who birthed him; the number
was huge, of course, but not nearly as great
    as the number of ants alive in the world
right now, or the billions of bacteria inside
    anyone's body. And his figures suggested
these early people still live inside us,
    grunting their cave-man observations, tasting
the wind tinged with the ichors of long-lost
    creatures who moved like that wind, with light
in their eyes, like ours, creatures that tasted
    so delicious we ate them into oblivion, as merely
by living we extended the great chain of human
    fuckers passed down from that first birth, all
those dreams and hungers leading to *now*
    and on into the future—or veering off slightly
to the side, ignoring what we think of as the *future*
    for something more like the *peripheral*—a river
that branches like a web as it falls, to nurture
    so many different kinds of being,
each with its own way of making a world.
    And then he was quoted as saying how everything
is language and everything speaks, even
    grasses and trees, to make itself real
to itself. Just a kid, still in high school, hardly
    old enough to shave, he claimed his calculations
were just an experiment he'd happened to find himself
    doing one rainy afternoon, instead
of his English homework, which was to finish
    The Scarlet Letter and write a short essay
on secrets and faith, or the vagaries of love.

The Edge of the World

Let's imagine a woman could walk to the edge
of the world as we know it, sit down there to rest
and look out over what we think of as nothing
while she waits for her husband to arrive with the supplies.
Or perhaps she doesn't wait and just keeps walking,
wondering whether she might simply disappear.
She's the kind of woman gives a dollar to the homeless guy
as though it's just a loan; she's the kind of person
who gathers up stray cats and takes them to the pound
so the wild birds will be safe in her garden.
Now she walks into nothing at the edge of the world,
and it's not what you'd expect from the stories of conquistadores
hacking out the jungle for its gold. No, she finds herself
sitting in a café drinking cappuccino
and talking to someone who looks like he could be
a door into a room full of light, in a house
so perfect she'd dissolve there, or explode like tiny bubbles
in a glass of champagne, as her husband stands confused
back at the edge there, calling her name
until he gives up, turns around and goes home
to find someone like her, someone he doesn't know
though everything about her is familiar, as though
he'll never wake again. And so he lives by dreaming.

The Mica-Daughter

Sure, we could ask our *true selves* to slice open
the clouds hanging in our closets, and let
the memories of summer afternoon thunderstorms
sweeten our shoes; we could throw open our windows
to let the waves rush in; sure, we could awaken
the surfboards sleeping in their narrow cots
and ride from wind to breeze to breath—

or we could practice the instruments we've never
mastered: tweezers and dental floss, toothbrush
and broken-toothed comb; we could learn how to stroke
harmonics by grooming our middle-aged physiognomies

if it weren't for afternoons like this one, when a man
called father gets caught in the window, and fades
into something like the skin of our eyes as we watch
the trees fill with dusk and the cars move their passengers
up and down the streets, when we can't help seeing
a crow who looks like our mother out there
nodding at the window. But then she's just a stump
by the time we arrive. It's like the smell of glass
in winter, a mirror filled with frozen rain,

as the brother, our brother, holds something like a howl
inside his shadow. Soon enough he's only
the smell of a tooth buried under a pillow
by a wolf-child with an old soul, the son who sings
pop songs backward and is chosen as a holy man
by his crossing guard, his teachers, and his friends, yet his friends
are afraid of the charms he weaves with the wind
to make himself something like grass-kneeling-down,
long hair of the bodies imprisoned underground,

as you are imprisoned in the girl of this family,
Sweet Sally of the Almost-There, who glistens like mica
and breaks things to mend them, to break them and mend them
again by stitching or gluing, staples
or nails. When you clap she'll vanish. But listen:
truly she has never been; truly, she is mica
at the center of our days, that sharpens our bones
and lights those faces in the photograph albums
we consult to remember our lives, until eventually

we've misplaced what glinted. By then we're just lost light.

The Horses

In that place you never want to talk about, there were
horse skins hanging from nails in the barn
where there once had been horses. You told me your parents

would go in there sometimes and strip each other naked
and slip into those horse skins. You've said their bodies
would seem to grow larger to fill that slack skin

until they were actual horses. And you stood there
in the bare yard waiting for those horses to push open
that barn door with their massive heads and limp off

as though they were overworked and world-weary, out
into the tall grass; their ribs showed gaunt,
their eyes were filmy, and flies made a dark cloud

around their slack bodies, but still they walked out there
while you aired-out the barn, gathered their clothing,
folded it neatly, and set it in a pile

on the bench for later. Then you went inside
to nap and wander through the house. You cooked yourself
a big meal—something you loved—and then you waited

for the moon to rise full through the still afternoon.
And that night you would carry out the saddles and reins,
bit and blinders, or you'd walk out

in your nightgown to ride your mother and father
bareback, until they remembered who they were
by the feel of your small legs around them.

To Blow Away like Mist

A man I knew felt sometimes as though a dog
was stuck inside his body, almost as large as he was—
black lab or golden retriever—unable
to move in that cramped dark, yet waiting for something,
listening to the sounds outside him, in the world.

When humans were lost in the rubble of disasters,
dogs like his inner life worked tirelessly—
beyond exhaustion, even to the point of death—
to save the victims, or locate their bodies.
The man knew he wasn't gifted with such vivid selflessness,
that he lacked the keen senses such heroic dogs need.
This realization opened a great emptiness inside him:

he could let himself seem to blow away then, like mist
in tall grass at dawn before anyone's walked there
or even looked out at it, when the day's breeze rises
and each blade of grass is lifted into clarity,
each stalk standing more taut as it dries,

and the small birds swoop down to disappear there for a moment
then swirl themselves up into the unencumbered sky.

Nature Poem

*I'm wondering how to fill it, that sack you left me
of sky, redundant as an egg . . .*
                    —Bill Berkson

Something like a swarm of bees inside the air,
        something like a mattress full of quills, or a tee shirt
                glistening with fish scales sloughed from the body
        of a man who blistered his fingers on the clouds
he leaped to grab onto, as though he could become them,
        so he could be rainfall. This is the grief
                of wool hats in the tropics, or a bone in the river,
        that's been smoothed into a pebble. You pick it up and wonder
what the wind might intend as it worries the trees—

        but wind intends nothing, of course, like that pebble
                falling through the ocean inside you, behind your
        rib bones and moon-bone and closets full of blaring
ambulance-street-cars and broken fire trucks
        hoping to rescue the snakes from your shoes
                before they start sliding up your legs like vines
        to poke into your holes. So I lean to read your palm,
close enough to smell that perfume you've sprayed
        on your clothes and hair as though that might make you
                less mortal. And it does, at least while the fevers
        are rising inside us and our fingers are stroking
that fur; at least while our barefoot dances
        continue long after the music's gone limp
                and the rain has reminded us again of the silence

        always inside, like the lake we dive into,
so crowded the with arm-length ravenous fish
        we think of as *sheriffs of the ocean*, though
                they're caught here in fresh water, sluggish with thirst
        and yearning for salt. But we let them devour us
anyway, the way a man might turn into
        the cat he petted, and purr his way into
                oblivion while his wife sat at home

watching old sitcoms and picking at her fingernails
until they were bleeding, then doing pushups
     until she broke down and cried out   *dirt*
       will be dirt.   Remember: those fish weren't fooled
    by the flies you tied with your father, leaning
in the near-dark basement workroom, while
      your mother took her clothes off in the kitchen upstairs,
         lay down on the floor and dreamed she might melt
into a skeleton to demonstrate just how

a fish might shiver. Soon there was glittering
     glass in the path you walked, barefoot,
        thinking you might still escape the relentless
     dogs in your body—large dogs that howled
like wolves and were always ravenous, until
     your bare feet left blood prints all over the floor
        beside your mother, while your father took a shower
    and sang in the voice of Ella Fitzgerald
or Bessie Smith, if they could have sung
     like a man who sang like a woman, off key,
        and the walls started sweating as the rain seeped through
    the wallpaper your mother had hung, pictures
of fruits that have never existed, and carrots,
     interspersed with small mammals—bunnies and squirrels—
       cute creatures, while off in the distance the farmhouse
    waited so patiently it almost made you cry
as the horses and pigs there exploded, one by one.

The Pond

If I claimed I grew up in a house made real
by the songs my father sang as he moved
from room to room, songs he made up
to make the furniture solid and keep
the windows holding the wind, and if I
told you I sat in my room and cried
when he fell silent at last, I'd have to
sing in my own voice to fill up the silence
he left us, if I wanted to keep things
whole—and I know so few songs that are *mine*,
and I know the whole house is listening.
So I start singing, just singing, and the songs
begin to move like breeze through the house.
If I told you my brother is dancing as he listens,
in the bedroom we share, my sister chattering
to keep my voice distant, my mother would be lying
in bed, dreaming of holding my father,
who slept like a hole in the ground beside her,
a cave that filled slowly with pure water when it rained—
cool, refreshing curtains of wetness
falling as we slept, to fill up the emptiness
gaping beside her and make a small pond
we could swim in, together again,
whenever that rain stopped falling.

The Truth of Poetry

We were walking through an unfamiliar neighborhood, carrying
a wolf's heart in a basket and looking at the street signs.
There were clouds of dragonflies darkening the sky,
so we felt like we were walking through twilight, though
it was only early afternoon. We'd heard that a wolf's heart

might keep beating for years, and that it might be sewn
into our bodies with no more pain
than a tattoo or a piercing. We imagined we might be made
more nearly immortal if the skin of this heart
were woven into ours, but by the time we found the address
of the veterinarian, the heart

had stopped beating in my hands, and my girlfriend had slipped
into the subway to go home to her family
for dinner. So I carried that dead heart alone
through the city, practicing the many ancient languages

of howling. But silently: I was lost now
and didn't want anyone to find me.

The Hike

I decided to walk a big circle that day
to see what I could see. It felt good to have a body
after weeks at the desk; it felt good to saunter
alone, not talking except in my head,
maybe singing a little. If there were crows
cawing I'd reply, I thought, and if a deer
watched from the trees, maybe I would see it,
as I knew I'd see breezes moving through the grasses,
as I knew I'd see spiderwebs. Maybe I'd sit down
and read or write a little. If I could just open
myself a little wider, I thought, I might be something
instead of just someone, for a little while.
I might even try to stand still for an hour,
or lie down off the path where no one could see me
and pretend to dry up and blow away. I could be
a gesture signaling through the trees. Watch me
move as emptiness through the energetic air
like a glint you didn't see, but you thought you did.

The Windows

Everything's a window the professor told my class,
and I thought about breaking that glass, or shutting
the curtains—or better yet opening those windows
and climbing out into the snowy world beyond.
He said fashioning windows *is the only way*
we can make sense of what we see, so even
as I walked off through that snow I must have made windows.
Pretty soon I found a road, plowed clean and gleaming black,
between those walls of snow, and I walked, not the least bit
chilly, imagining I would find something
eventually. And soon a big dog came bounding up.
I smelled wood smoke. Imagine discovering a village
full of people who seem to know you, at the end
of a long road, out in a wilderness of snow!
I stepped inside a house whose first floor was a dark bar,
warm and crowded with bearded men
who raised their glasses as I entered, beckoned me
to sit by the fire, and asked if I was having
the usual. I'd been lonely forever
I realized as the barmaid brought my soup and beer
with a wink that felt genuine. I was starving, so I ate
without stopping, through the night, and then I slept, in a room
with curtained windows behind which many birds
were singing, as though teaching me another way to wake.

Big Bend

Driving through the desert, we think of the children
deciding to lie down for a rest, holding hands.
We wonder at their parents. We are driving to the river,
cool and relaxed, squinting in the early sun
despite our dark glasses. We want to touch the river,
maybe wade there, lie down in the cool water
and let ourselves be carried down river. We want to
echo our voices against the canyon walls.
We think of the children, and their parents, setting out
across the wide desert, still cool and dripping
from crossing the river. Sheep graze on the other side
as we sit in the shade of the canyon, cool
from the river though the day's already burning
and somewhere the children are walking, holding hands,
thinking of the river, their parents, and home
as they look across the desert and seem to see a river
quivering the air like a dream. We are driving,
cool and refreshed and talking of our plans
for when we get home from the desert; we are listening
to music or news of what's happened far away
but we're thinking of the river and the canyon, and of
the children walking slowly, holding each other
across the wide desert, alone.

Dream of Myself as an Only Child

I was heading outside to play in the rain
which had been falling for days, when my mother
called from her bath. She was reading and needed
a towel for her book. The bubbles, like blisters
around her body, were frothy and blue,
and their sweet scent made me think of an animal
caught in the body of a person who'd been sleeping
too long to be human anymore, someone
who might have turned over on his side while he slept
and simply disappeared. So I closed the bathroom door
and went out to wander the sidewalk, collecting
worms that had drowned in the rain, searching
for dry spots on the front stoops to leave them for the birds,
as the trains flew by underground. I watched
the puddles shiver and imagined my father
down there, coming home; he was dozing, dreaming
of some other life and would sleep through his stop,
while my mother emerged from her bath to wander
the apartment in robe and perfume, waiting,
as I waited for the birds to notice the worms
I'd left them, and the puddles disappeared, into
the ground while the evening erased things, one by one.

The House

She folds a piece of typing paper
into a house. Let's live here, she says,
as she makes herself tiny. I follow, and we enter

lives that feel suddenly new, surrounded
by walls and ceiling so drenched in light
we squint as we look at each other.

Our new house lacks windows, so we watch the walls
for shadows. Soon we'll have to scissor some doors
so we can move around outside again

but for now we're content with each other and the white
walls and our shadows against the white walls,
which move as though we were dancing.

Starting from Sleep

She tells me our bodies are nets dropped into
the ocean. And when they are pulled up, the minnows
are spilled out to flip-flop and strangle.

And then we are tossed back over, to dream:

> *I talk,* she says, *to my great-great-grandchildren*
> *by treating all things with whatever compassion*
> *I've drawn from the grace I've been shown. And those children*
> *thank me, and dream of being born.*

The wild parts of everything are disappearing everywhere.

Wood grain faint fingerprint
      pores eyes blue breathing
wind dust mind afternoon
    tide lips   and sudden flowers.

The Journey Home

When I finally summoned the urge to go home
after all these years, I couldn't remember
exactly how to get there, though I did know how to find
the train. I filled a bag with small gifts
for all the old friends, though I couldn't remember
exactly who they were—what I mean is I couldn't
remember who'd died: chocolate and nice-smelling
soap, things everyone loves. I was dreaming
already of how they would all blush and clap
to see who I was now. There were no empty seats,
so I stood. Presently someone got up
and hurried from the car, then another jumped up,
then two more, and so on until the train
was empty, though of course all those slobs
had left their garbage behind—cups
and newspapers, wrappers of who knows what.
So I leaned down the aisle picking up their junk,
I kneeled down and swept it from under their seats,
marveling at all the good stuff they'd chucked.
Then I sat down to read the old newspapers I'd piled
beside me on the seat, my ticket safely tucked
into my front pocket, as the lights flickered
and the doors finally slid shut, sighing.
The train gave a shiver then as though it felt the cold.
It groaned like it knew something I didn't. You know
the kind of groan I mean? *No train can make that sound,*
you're probably thinking. But you are very wrong.
And soon we were moving through the darkness.

Selections from
The Mica Mine

Wolves

I'm reading a book about wolves that never
actually discusses the animals but instead
delves into twigs and paths, bloody
entrails, livestock, and frightened families

and while I'm reading, a cloud of mosquitoes
hovers but doesn't bite; a crow lands in the grass
and yells at me to wake up, as though I'd been sleeping

while a phone starts ringing in the distance, but I don't
want to get up to answer, since this wolf-book
seems to be growing warm in my lap
like a plate of glowing coals I must carry through the night

to my comrades, so they will have fire.

Another Animal

Forget about forgiveness: There's another kind of animal
at your door, so you don't have to make up lists
and fancy equations to impress the family
still sleeping in the house behind you. There are many ways
to step outside, and just as many to step back

to let that animal enter, yawning
and asking for coffee. There are many ways of being
half dressed in your nakedness as you stand in the morning
with all the little birds sleeping in your ears
and all the perfect creatures sleeping now inside the bleeding

wound no suture could mend. It's like a river
that spills beyond its banks, rises to a flood,
then subsides into itself again. That animal is nothing
like a pet although you feed it from a bowl, although you take it
for walks and let it curl up at your feet

at night, except when it moves around outside
and carries the dark in its fur as it shakes itself
like a dusty rug; it whimpers as it sleeps
while you listen to the life that is only partly yours
breathing inside you. But this animal would save you

if the house were to fall down around you, even
if you were dead inside it would save you, even
if that meant it would die too it would save you, or at least
it would try to. It doesn't have a name, but it's all yours.
Open your door now, stand back and let it in.

Sky

Who took the chance to leave home with only
the clothes she was wearing, and someone else's name.

Who took the chance
to sleep without a blanket
in the litter-filled woods by the highway, in the rain:

Who closed her eyes
and slept while the delicate
animals sniffed her, and ravenous insects

by the millions slipped under her skin as she mumbled
a little in her dream. *Did no one look for her?*

Someone walks barefoot through the city in the dark,
a delicate woman with aching teeth
whose bones have been arranged like kindling, to burn.

We wake to the smell of smoke, and look up at the sky.

The Hive

Someone else's loss, buzzing through the garden
like the bee that got under your shirt and landed
in your chest hair but didn't sting; someone's grief
right there like a stone in the almost-raining afternoon
with the smell of horse-sweat and mowed grass and hot
asphalt. You held my hand as we stood
at the fence and called to those horses, and felt
the first raindrops and smelled the cooling road.
Someone else's tragedy passing like an awkward truck
climbing our dirt road, unbalanced by the dead woman's
bulky furniture, and the potholes. Someone else
looking out her window at the strangers standing
on the road squinting at her door as though
expecting it to open, then walking slowly on.
Down the hill, trucks rip out the clear-cut tree stumps
and we think of the coyote who slunk across our yard
with a squirrel in its jaws, and we think of the bears
at our garbage. There were birds calling out like children
playing hide-and-seek, pretending to be hurt
somewhere deeper in the woods, and you tell me you love me
like fingernails, like hair; you love me like breath
when you're sleeping, wrapped up in dust while the crows
in our closets make darkness from the clothes we never wear
and our bodies start crying out in languages the trees
might dance to, as though we were singing.

I Wake

in the middle of the night to something moving
across the porch outside our bedroom,
sliding furniture around
and muttering. It's raining, but I'm sure I hear footsteps,

so I hold myself still. The sprigs of flowering
dogwood my wife has collected glow
in the moonlight, by the window; she snores peacefully
beside me. I'm naked. Today a red-tailed hawk

swooped across our garden, to vanish in the woods
before I was sure what I saw, so
I didn't say anything. Later, we had dinner
with a friend who's grown suddenly old, and as

we said our goodbyes, she told us again
about the day her husband left her,
out of the blue, when her adult children
were toddlers. *It hasn't stopped hurting,* she said
as she closed her front door. Driving home, I noticed

my wife was crying, face turned to the window.
I thought of pulling over, reaching out, asking her
to tell me what was wrong, but that road is difficult
to follow at night, and I wasn't even sure

she was crying, after all, when I looked over again,
so I drove on in silence, keeping my eyes
on the road, respecting that darkness.

It Was

hunger for the muck at low tide, for the rain
filled with its afterlife: dust and flecked skin,
hunger for the marrow, the compost and the mulch,
the damp leaves just starting to rot: the evening

cool like the air in the cellar where we listened
to the adults stomping above us; we could hear
the hunger in their voices, so we climbed out, past the jars
and what looked like bones in that darkness; we hungered

for something like fresh-cut grass and pine,
pond ice just melting, the touch on the wrist
that makes something ache: your body is real;
your shoes are small caves full of everywhere you've walked.

There are mirrors in your memory; you think of them as rain
and mirrors that think they are windows: *look out
at the lost world* they'd say. If mirrors could talk

that hurt dog would run all night beside the train
in a snowstorm, to wake as a man in the morning
with a pure-white landscape in his brain. If he walks out,

it's hunger he's walking through, deep snow; it's hunger
if he stops at a meadow in the snow and imagines
he won't own himself by morning. He's culled
who he is now from who he used to be

as he stands there so patiently, learning how to melt
as a way of embracing the ground.

The Fireflies

Carpenter bees drill steadily into
the beam above my head, making perfect holes,
leaving neat piles of sawdust.

A butterfly lands on the sill beside my coffee cup.

In the shade, mosquitoes caught in spiderwebs
buzz and fall silent. It hasn't rained for weeks.

Last night, we watched thousands of fireflies
rise into the sky, so many they looked
like desert constellations, except they were moving
like music. We were visiting friends,
drinking wine. A few of us were dancing.

Later, I woke alone in the dark,
got up and wandered through the quiet house
looking for you, who were sitting outside
in the garden, in your pale summer nightgown.

I watched you for a while, then went back to bed
where I lay glowing, like an insect full of light

or a miniscule glint in the teeming night sky
thousands of light years away.

This Melody (excerpt)

1.

moved through our bodies
    and taught us not to think

        which taught us to open
         our bodies to the grass

at the edge of those unexplained woods where the deer
    stood without names

         quivering
         and taught us

      to lie down and open
        ourselves
        and learn to

            sleep
            again

            like the boulders.

2.

Wake up! my father
would call on those chilly

mornings when my body
was somehow more dense

than it is now, and I could sleep for days,

growing my fur,
dreaming my life,

wondering when I'd be born, and what

I'd call myself
when I stopped pretending

and let what I feared come inside me.

3.

I'd like to carry myself away
      myself, not let you
carry me

        but the day is so full
           of gleaming, and the breezes

         are moving so slyly
    through the trees, I feel

alone forever,
as though forever

        were alive
     like a body—

so I give myself to you.

4.

For generations, their dead were buried
      on top of each other, like mica-flecks or wounds.

    We think they knew   the dead still dream
        for years beyond their lives; we think

they knew dreams push upward
          like stones do, toward the light
    while roots push deeper into darkness.

Imagine dreams rising from the old dead through the new—

      hummingbird wings
    woven like veils
      across their empty eyes.

5.

The first dreams were trees
   he explained to us then,

whose leaves were pressed
      into oil and charcoal.

    They contained a secret knowledge
    only angels ever sang.

6.

In a room of rubble
and brittle light,

    I suddenly know things
    I'll never understand:

each moment is a living
animal, leaping

    sunlight
    to give us

these bodies.

7.

—all the shells on the beach,
    all the ripped-up seaweed

        teeming with tiny lives:

        the clothes you wear
    as though they hadn't
been made by children,
    as though they made you shine:

the breaths you will waste, all the heartbeats.

8.

The moon
rises

    like a moth
      into the darkness

    inside us, full of satellites
mapping out our lives.

9.

Birdsong, older
than science or the prayers

        oak leaves rustle
        as they color into fall:

    the song of my mother's
    labored breath

as I wait without knowing
to be born.

10.

He told us his parents
        were angels who lived
                in the branches outside
        his bedroom.

They whispered and tapped
        at his window when he slept,
                so he climbed out and sat
        in that tree for a while

with his parents, and looked at the moon.

11.

All day the smell of rain-drenched boulders

        and when I moved,
        something moved in the distance—

something wild, off beyond the trees.

        Touch me deeper,
        she said, than language,
                and we will turn to ash

                together, naked
        before each other,

alive in the strangeness
of burning.

12.

House of swans and moonlight,
       small room of down and blankets, closets

            cluttered with sweaty
shoes filled
         with the husks of crickets.

      Outside, moths like bottle rockets
rise into the dusk, which stops growing darker

         and just sits there, waiting to be breathed.

13.

I walked out naked
    with morning, lonely
        as a bone
        and stood
like a moment of light,

as my other body,
    the one that floats
        to the surface, stirred
        in the bed, and I heard

     someone singing
     in the kitchen, a song
       I sing too,
when I'm happy to be waking

     on a rainy autumn morning
     with nobody to please.

14.

Teach me the names
        of those bones in our bodies
                that carry the weight
        of whatever we've denied;

train me to hear
        the roots of the oaks
                as they spread out into
        the darkness, as they

reach around stones
        and all those other
                heavy buried objects; help me

        listen to the water dripping in caves
hundreds of years underground.

15.

All that night
birds flew through my bedroom.

        Their wings were like whispers
        in a country without air,

that country we left to be born, and they never

        landed, as far as I know, since they had
        such a great distance
                to travel.

16.

We were drifting across the huge lake, almost
out of sight, finally, diving in sometimes

to scatter the fish, content in our nakedness,

hoping we'd soon see the far shore we'd heard
so much of
in our other lives,

where the angels lived.

19.

Morning light—

day by itself—
a door you might glide through:

light that might walk

if sound could yearn,
which is singing, that yearning;

when the day comes, no one
will meet you, no one

will have a name for you—
and so you'll be just air.

20.

Someone tries singing for days without stopping
  or making a sound, like sap does, rising.

Another tries sleeping beneath the snow
  in a country whose language is silence.

        I took the same train for years, back and forth
          from a station full of people
              I thought of as myself
        to a station full of people
              that looked like other animals.

    The whole time I pretended I lived outside my body.
    The whole time I imagined I was myself alone.

        Our fur in that other life
          was matted, flecked with rain.

  21.

        And the million creatures
            that haven't yet been named,
  and the languages that haven't been discovered, ways
      of being fully charged
            that haven't yet been known—

they are also vanishing:

            a rain so soft and cool
          birds shimmer as they fly, beaks open for the taste
      that teaches new songs, and new ways to land

  in the cool damp grass
            where the inner life is clean—

54.

When the body of a young girl
        who died a thousand years ago
is discovered in the marl, with a scrap of the shawl
        she was wearing that day, a day like any other—

when her bones are gathered and placed in the glass case
        for anyone to look at, and wonder:

        The pregnant woman next door sings a lullaby
to her unborn baby, while she sweeps her patio.

And here's another miracle: She doesn't know I'm listening.

55.
                . . . live oaks whisper to the light
as it moves through their branches. Their shadows whisper too
        like dust falling through an empty closet
                in a house that's been abandoned for years.

And in a house down the street an old lady has a dream
        of an open window filled with falling snow

                and a husband in an empty field, disguised as a tree
which whispers to the morning as it lightens.

56.
          Walls made of light, like paper lamps or snow,
     windows thickened with winter's icy dandruff—

          someone in a room down the hall calls out
     in sleep, like a sudden gust of wind that scatters

the leaves you just raked up to burn; in this dusk-light
          they look like the skeletons of bats, or starving

     mice. When you pick one up and breathe across its lacy body,

it quivers and runs off
                    amazed to be alive.

57.
          . . . bodies frozen for thousands of years
     are discovered, some of whom still have faces
          and tongues, some of whom still have their innards.

     One newly-thawed body had foot-long fingernails.

Another was covered in his own hair, which had pushed
     through the woof and weave of his tunic
and cottoned him like a cocoon.

          Some of the stories they told, some
     of the food they ate,
          whatever songs they sang—

     She was wearing a necklace of finely-carved shells
a thousand miles from the sea. *Do you see me*
     at all? my wife asked last night before bed,

                    but I think I was already sleeping.

The Window

The girl who became my mother sits
    at a window in the morning watching a clutch
of brown birds fuss at an empty winter feeder.
    Her parents, in the background, scowl as they watch her

as though she'd betrayed them somehow. But we don't know
    that story. We do know she opens her window
to the quiet city street and waits for the birds
    to fly in; we do know that a man walking home

sees her there, so beautiful and young,
    and vows to meet her, and calls up *good morning*,
which scatters the birds. She pretends she hasn't heard him
    but calls back anyway, and waits for him to come.

The Distant Waterfall

The big bear appears at your living room window
so close you can study his pigeon-toed walk,
his delicate steps around the potted plants
on your back wall. He sniffs at the base of the dogwood
where you dump your morning coffee grinds; you watch him
cock his ears when he hears you, naked
behind the sliding glass door.

Now he moves up the slope across the garden, pausing
to sniff new flowers and slurp a quick drink
from the bird bath—he doesn't knock it over—then down
to the carport outside the garage where you stand now,
still naked, to watch him. There's a big bag of garbage

on the floor beside you: mussel shells and fish bones,
so you thump on the door and growl like the fearsome
old man you've suddenly become,

and he seems to believe you, turns away and saunters
up into the woods, back up into the mountains
just starting to green with spring, where you wandered
yesterday looking for the waterfall whose roar
you thought you could hear in the distance but never
seemed to get closer to, no matter how you bushwhacked
and listened, then bushwhacked again—until you realized

it was probably just the ringing in your ears or the distant
highway, or simply the beautiful place
you've imagined finding for yourself and your family
to visit and be happy, and you'd pretty soon be lost
if you kept on looking deeper, moving further off the trail.

The Skinny-Dip

After she wonders how psychic wounds
move, like genetics, from parent to child,
he muses on the way
a field of boulders
dance without moving, for millions of years—

and after they've silenced their breaths to listen
to a chirping in the undergrowth, they wonder how quickly
their senses might sharpen
if they bushwhacked off the trail
into the deep woods, to let themselves get lost—

which reminds them of people they've loved and lost
and prompts reminiscences
they both know by heart—

paths they might follow through the dark toward each other—

and when they come to a bend in the river
where a waterfall fills a dark pool, he undresses
and slips in, yelping; she laughs at his shivering
nakedness, then takes off her own clothes, to stand

leaning toward him, hands extended. Just in case.

The Legacy

All morning I've been collecting stones,
lugging them down from the woods to my garden
where I spread them out on the ground to admire
their shapes and glinting mica.

Then, as the afternoon sun warms us,
I fill a bucket with water and scrub them.
It takes until evening. When I grow tired,

I leave the stones drying, go inside,
pour some wine, and sit down to eat.

My wife and I watch TV and sit quietly
together; then we go to bed
and hug each other chastely through the night.

Tomorrow I'll carry each stone back into
the woods and lay it gently on the earth
where I found it, so no one else will know.

The Prayer

If you wander through the woods collecting stones
to border your garden, your path won't follow
logic, as might be the case if you were gathering
mushrooms or looking
for the quickest way home.

Some stones are so pale they glow in the woods-light;
others rest on last year's leaves
as though someone had carried them there
and set them down. Still others are so grubby

it's difficult to see what they'll look like
once they're clean. Lined up along the path,
they look pleased to be admired, and I do admire them
every time I walk there. I know stones sing

only perfect silence, like the stars, which is why
I carry them down through the woods, and why
I talk to them in my own language

as I hold them to my body,
as I lay them gently down.

Born in New York City and raised in its suburbs, Michael Hettich has lived in Colorado, Northern Florida, Vermont, Miami, and Black Mountain, North Carolina, where he now lives with his family. He holds a Ph.D. from the University of Miami and taught for many years at Miami Dade College where he was awarded an Endowed Teaching Chair. His poetry, essays, and reviews have appeared widely in many journals and anthologies, and he has published more than two dozen books of poetry across five decades. His honors include several Individual Artist Fellowships from the Florida Division of Cultural Affairs, The Tampa Review Prize in Poetry, the David Martinson/Meadowhawk Prize, a Florida Book Award, and the Lena M. Shull Book Award from the North Carolina Poetry Society. His website is michaelhettich.com